# Crazier
# THINGS
## HAVE HAPPENED

*The memoir of one woman's journey of survival
through the world of infertility and the discovery
of a life full of synchronicities and blessings!*

STACEY WEBBER

**BALBOA.**PRESS
A DIVISION OF HAY HOUSE

Balboa Press books may be ordered through booksellers or by contacting:

Balboa Press
A Division of Hay House
1663 Liberty Drive
Bloomington, IN 47403
www.balboapress.com
844-682-1282

Psalm139:13-18, New Revised Standard Version
Scripture quotations marked NRSV are taken from the New Revised Standard Version of the Bible, Copyright © 1989, by the Division of Christian Education of the National Council of the Churches of Christ in the United States of America. Used by permission. All rights reserved. Website

Print information available on the last page.

ISBN: 979-8-7652-4145-5 (sc)
ISBN: 979-8-7652-4147-9 (hc)
ISBN: 979-8-7652-4146-2 (e)

Library of Congress Control Number: 2023908065

Balboa Press rev. date: 04/27/2023

# CONTENTS

I would like to dedicate this book to my family.

To my husband, you are my rock. Thank you for always supporting and loving me unquestionably, and for always having faith in me and trusting me!

To my children, you are my whole heart, my reason for being, and I love you more than words can convey. May you always reach for your greatest dreams and know that you are so very loved!

To my brother, I am so proud of you. You are the best example of what a great person is, for your children and mine. An amazing brother, dad, and uncle, you are the most generous soul I know, and I am so thankful for you and your amazing children!

I also wrote this book in honor of my mom, my first and best friend, my confidant, and my biggest teacher. Thanks for always showing me that love is eternal!

To my first incredible editor, Sarah Lamb. You resonated with why I wanted to share my story, and I thank you for all your compassion and belief in the importance of getting my story out there, to help and encourage others on their own journeys. I'm forever grateful my instincts pulled me to you!

I am so thankful for everyone at Balboa Press, for all your hard work and dedication to make this book finally happen. Much love and appreciation to all!

I would also like to give a shout-out to my amazing acupuncturist, Shelley Kelley Sullivan, as you were also my therapist and confidant, and I can never thank you enough!

Also, to all my friends mentioned here by name or anonymously, you are also my family, and I'm so proud to have the support and strength of your friendships along this ride of life. You know who you are.

To my in-laws, sister-in-law, and nieces, you are all beautiful, and I love you!

To my cousin, Steph, I love you! You will never know how your conviction and strength inspired me that day, and still does.

Lastly, to all the doctors who are a part of our story, you know who you are, and I have nothing but love, respect, and appreciation for all of you!

# ACKNOWLEDGMENTS

I would like to thank authors Esther and Jerry Hicks, and Abraham, as well as the late and great Wayne Dyer, for their influences on me. I have read and studied all of them, and the spiritual messages they have conveyed have resonated wholeheartedly with me. If you are familiar with their teachings, I am sure you will pick up on their influences on my life as you read this book. I would like to thank these amazing souls for showing me the power of quieting my mind so I can hear my inner being, and for showing me that life is simply about the energy you give.

This morning, I found this quote in my inbox that I would like to share with you. Perfect timing, I would say! Just another synchronicity of life showing me how perfect divine timing is. Thank you!

> "Don't get lost in the diagnosis, the medicine, or in the statistics about what somebody else did about it. If you don't feel good, it's because you're not thinking in a way that allows the Energy to flow. You could just get really, really mad at someone you love and make every muscle in your body stiff. And you would ask, 'Why does my body feel this way?' And we say, because you've had a vibrational tug-of-war going on ... Stop looking for anything other than your mental and emotional state of being as answers to why you feel how you feel in your body. It is all vibrational—no exception! And when you get that, then it doesn't matter what diagnosis has been given to you—it doesn't matter—it's temporary."
> Our Love
> Esther (Abraham and Jerry)

And also, from the amazing Deepak Chopra, who has influenced my life with his incredible wisdom, here is a quote I recently came across: "You can believe the diagnosis, not the prognosis."

What this means to me is that doctors can only tell you how other people have handled a similar diagnosis, but no one knows you, your vibrational level, what you believe, and what you can conceive, because no one is exactly like you. Only you get to decide what you want to believe; only you have the power to believe what is possible for you! You do not have to limit your possibilities to what doctors or your parents or your family or other people believe. You get to control your power, and if you can conceive your desire, it is possible for you!

# INTRODUCTION

As far back as I can remember, I have always wanted to be a mom. This story is about my journey to motherhood and the many challenges I faced and overcame along the way. I have been pregnant seven times in a span of ten years on my journey to motherhood. I've gone through pregnancy, miscarriage, multiple intrauterine inseminations, multiple in vitro fertilizations, a blighted ovum, a tubular pregnancy, and the rare-disease diagnosis of a child. However, the joy of motherhood became possible for me and is my greatest blessing, even with all these challenges. I have also endured my own mortality and the physical loss of my mother; yet, she has continued to show me the eternalness of her love and how, through the lens of tears and laughter, life still is more blessed and whole than I ever imagined!

Through a fresh understanding of spirituality, science, and the power of belief, I encourage the reader to find his or her own path of truth, with anything that may challenge them, and not to just follow what I am saying. More than ever, women and couples are faced with fertility challenges. This book is a reminder to believe in the desire of motherhood calling to these women and couples, and to inspire them to have hope and faith and trust in themselves and their dreams. It is also a book to remind you that, no matter what challenges or life circumstances you may be going through, there is a stronger, more self-empowered you on the other side.

No matter what challenges come your way in life, choose to follow your heart, because a life lived from love instead of from fear is the most beautiful life one can live! Leave the fear behind, and focus on the love. What we put our attention on will increase, so increase attention on what you want and how you want things to be. Live from love!

I hope others who hear my story will be encouraged to follow their own heart, that they will learn to not give up, but to learn to trust their inner voice and know that anything is possible for them. Through this journey, I have learned what I believed, what worked for me, what did not work, and why. I learned how our beliefs and desires shape our lives. I figured out how to tune into my own thoughts and desires and have a positive outlook. I tuned into the many miracles, or synchronicities, and "winks" from the universe along the way, as can anyone. And I'm still learning. Although it sometimes was in hindsight, perhaps the most important thing I have learned is to trust myself! I hope you enjoy!

# TO THE READER

While reading this book, I recommend taking a pause at the end of each chapter to reflect on something in the reader's own life that relates to the subject matter of the chapter. The reader should try to have some self-reflection, because many times, it is only after something has happened that we can go back and understand the how or the why of it all!

I hope for the reader, while diving into my story, that they will learn from my experiences to listen to their inner being and trust their own intuition. Also, I hope the reader gains a bigger picture of what some women's journeys to motherhood are, and to just be more open-minded, because you never know what other people are going through. If we can pass on tuning into our own intuition to the next generation, and as a society, if we can be less judgmental and more understanding and compassionate, we could have a much more caring and loving world for our children to inherit. It is up to us individually to look for the good in all things, and to see the many blessings along life's journey.

# DONATIONS

A $1 donation from every book sold will be given to https://www.
fodsupport.org/, the support group that helped us and continues to help
families navigate the very challenging and frightening diagnosis of a fatty
oxidation disorder. Thank you, Deb Lee Gould for all you do for so many.
Please visit the website to learn more.

## CHAPTER 1

# Becoming a Mom for the First Time

* * * * * * * * *

Becoming a mother for the first time was slightly challenging. I thought I could just go off birth control, and it would happen. Well, after being on oral contraceptives for ten years, I probably should have first asked a few questions of my doctor or my mom. However, I was blissfully ignorant and thought I would just stop taking them. Not such a great idea in hindsight!

The first month we tried, we had been living together for four years and had been married for about a month. It did not happen, and I just about lost my mind. Looking back, I think I was so emotional because I had stopped the oral contraceptive medicine cold turkey, and my hormones were all over the place. When I realized I was not pregnant, I broke down in an emotional mess and called my mom. She gave me some of the best advice ever. Basically, she said, "Get your shit together, girl!" Mom told me to just relax and calm down. I was not being punished by a god, or anything else like that. Let my body chill out, give my husband back the fun-loving, happy girl he had married, and stop being a crazy person! So I listened. After all, she was my mom and had been married for twenty-seven years to Dad (although they were divorced at that point). She'd had my older brother and me when she was in her early twenties, and she was a great mom.

The next month, I was pregnant and over-the-moon ecstatic! My husband took a little longer to get excited. Don't get me wrong; he was glad about starting our own family, but he'd experienced a tumultuous relationship with his own dad, and he definitely had some misgivings to work out in his own mind. Luckily for him, he'd have nine months to get his shit together, too!

At nine weeks' gestation, I was in for a routine check. I had felt great. Everything was going ahead without any issues, but the nurse was having one. She moved the heart monitor around on my stomach a few times, unable to find the heartbeat! "It's OK," she said. "Sometimes the baby is just hiding. The baby could just be in a bad position to pick it up, but we need to be sure."

Be sure? Be sure of what? That my baby was just playing hide-and-seek, and it wasn't something worse? Not something unmentionable, unimaginable, or something horrible? That he or she was still alive? WTF! I drove myself home from that appointment in tears and shock and basically freaking out. Could I panic now? Was it OK to lose my shit? It was so damn scary, and I was all by myself, barely able to see where I was driving because of the streams of tears and the heart-wrenching, aching feeling in my chest. *This cannot be happening*, I kept thinking. *He or she is just hiding. It has to be! It must be, because for me, there is no other choice!* I felt fine. As the nurse had sent me home, she'd said, "This happens sometimes." I had to have faith. I can't remember what I did during that time, but I do remember how I felt. It was so devastating. In such a short time, I had gone from the highest of highs to the lowest of lows that I had known up until that point in my life!

We eventually were scheduled for an ultrasound, and there it was! The baby had been hiding, and it was perfectly normal. What a relief! Holy crap. What a shitty ride that was! However, it was still too soon to determine the baby's gender, and we had agreed we did not want to know, anyhow. This was our first child. It would be nice to have a surprise at the birth. The rest of the pregnancy was, as they say, uneventful—the type of pregnancy we all want to have!

It was the beginning of April, and in New England, we were having an April Fools' Day snowstorm. My brother was over for dinner, and I started to have contractions. My husband and brother thought I was playing an April Fools' joke on them because they did not believe I was going into labor. I sat on the couch, timing the contractions, and remembering I had heard stories of low barometric pressure in the atmosphere inducing labor. Thinking we may have to head to the hospital in a snowstorm was an overwhelming thought. Thankfully, they subsided, and it was four days later at home when I felt what I thought was my water breaking. We headed to the hospital, but the doctors were not convinced that it was amniotic fluid. It was my first time going into labor, and it can be hard to know if you are peeing or leaking amniotic fluid, since it's not always a gush. They decided to put me, my giant belly, and my husband up overnight in a single hospital bed. (They were out of cots.) Needless to say, neither one of us got much sleep.

Once the morning came, they did a litmus paper test to double-check if it was urine or amniotic fluid. It came back that, yes, it was amniotic fluid, and my water was broken. Since it was my first time giving birth, they wanted to see how my body would handle it on its own, and they tried to just let me labor. It was going on twenty-four hours since my water had broken, and I was not advancing to the next stage of labor on my own. No contractions, nothing. That's when they decided to fully "break the bag," as that sometimes gets things going. Out came a giant, crochet needle-looking thing. I'm not gonna lie; it was quite frightening! They broke the bag fully, but still no contractions. By now, the doctors were getting concerned because, since my water was broken, I could get bacteria in there and an infection if we waited too long to deliver the baby. This is when they decided to give me some Pitocin, which is medicine given through an IV to make your body start contractions.

The nurse set up the IV while the doctor was still in the room. Nothing had kicked in yet when the doctor said she had to go check on something and would be right back. Now it was just me and my husband waiting in the room. Suddenly, my stomach rolled like an ocean wave from the top on down, and I knew I had not made my stomach move like that.

I looked at my husband and asked, "Did you see that?"

He replied, "Yeah."

I looked him dead in the eyes and said, "Well, I didn't do that!"

It felt like my body was possessed. I didn't know if it was the baby or the medicine or what. All I knew was that something was happening, and my body had acted on its own. You know how you have a thought to move your arm before you move it, and the thought sends the message to your body, and then your body responds? Well, my brain had no thoughts, and my body just moved on its own.

I was still looking at my husband and said, "You need to get someone *now* 'cause I didn't do that!"

His face showed an expression of shock. He did not want to leave me alone, but he was also the only one there who could go get someone to help.

Luckily, the doctor and nurses were right outside the door. They all came in immediately and were in shock. My body had gone from zero to ten centimeters in a matter of seconds. Time to dial that stuff back! As it turned out, my body just needed a little nudge to get it going, but they had given me a great, big shove. Now I was in full-blown labor, and things were moving along quite rapidly. I had said I didn't want an epidural, and it was a good thing, because now there was no time for one!

Joseph Paul made his debut on his due date, April 6, arriving at seven pounds, nine ounces, and 21.25 inches long. We should have known then that he was going to love sports because he high-fived the doctor as he entered the world! When his father saw him for the first time, all he could say was, "He's so big!" It is amazing how they fit into such tight quarters.

Joseph was beautiful! Steely blue eyes, just like his dad, and we gave him his dad's name for his middle name, too. My husband is already a junior, so we wanted to pass on his name but still let our son have his own identity at the same time. It was a blessing and a relief that he was finally here, and we were so excited to be his parents. Little did we know at the time that the uneventfulness of the last few months was the calm before the storm!

Everything we had just gone through would be a cakewalk compared to what was coming. Parenthood would be the biggest blessing and scariest f—ing thing we would ever go through!

I often think of Garth Brooks's song, "The Dance," when I think back to before we decided to have children. I know Garth wrote it more about a couple, but it completely applies to how I feel about my journey to parenthood and my life in general. I am glad I didn't know and left my life to chance. Yes, I could have missed the pain, but the dance is the good stuff of life, and it is so worth it! If someone had told me all the challenges we were about to face, I think I'd have said maybe I didn't want to go there. But now, having gone through it, I am so glad we did, and I'm so glad for those challenges because we so appreciate life and all the little things most people take for granted. I now could not imagine my life being different, and I wouldn't want it to be. You can appreciate more when you know how truly blessed you are and how close you came to not having it! (If you are not familiar with his song, go look up the lyrics, you'll get what I mean!)

---- C H A P T E R  2 ----

# Joseph's Story

• • • • • • • • •

Joe was born two weeks before our first wedding anniversary. We had the usual three-day stay at the hospital when giving birth and then headed home. At the time, I was running an in-home day care, so I had closed for just three weeks to get my bearings again after giving birth. On our first anniversary, my in-laws came over to watch the baby so we could go out to eat, and I made Paul tell his mom everything, like she hadn't raised three kids on her own (and they all even survived)!

At dinner, I was wearing the maternity dress I had worn to my baby shower. We had said not to get each other anything, so Paul apparently took me literally, and when I handed him a card, he looked at me and said, "I thought we weren't getting each other anything?" I think I started crying right there at the table. I got up and excused myself to the bathroom and realized I had bled through the double pads I was wearing and onto my dress. Lovely! Now I was crying even more! We had nothing to talk about. We had focused on the pregnancy and the baby for the last year, and suddenly we were left to stare at each other and try to come up with something else to talk about besides the baby. Good luck with that!

We were different people now; we were parents, and our entire identities had changed. Well, I know I talked about the baby at least a couple of times, plus the times I asked Paul to call his mom, and that was no less than twice in the hour and a half we were "enjoying" dinner on the harbor, in the next town over. How did we get here, and who was this man sitting across the table from me? I may not have been sure of what I knew then, but I would eventually come to find out that this was the most loving, caring, kind, and supportive friend and husband I'd ever come to know. Even if he got me nothing for our first anniversary—and will argue to this day that he was just listening to what I had said by not getting me anything. Sure, that's the time you pick to listen?

The trials and tribulations of life's journey are really a magical ride, even if at the time we can't see it as such. I was so pissed off at that moment in time. My entire identity had changed, and I questioned not only who I was but who we were. I was so devastated. How could he not get me anything? Now I just look back and laugh at how stupid we both were. Him for not getting me anything, and me for being so upset. None of it mattered in the big picture. I know that now.

Joe's first year had a few changes for us, but we were loving every minute of it with him. Well, almost. Joe was a happy baby, but he did not sleep great, and as I was nursing him and up all night, I was exhausted. Nothing completely prepares you for those endless, sleep-deprived nights, not even all-nighters in college! After about two months, I gave my notice to the day-care families. I had started an in-home day care because I love kids, and I thought it would be a great way to get to stay home with my own kids and provide a safe, loving environment for the children of friends, family, and neighbors, all while provide financially for my own family as well. But I just couldn't get past this overwhelming feeling that I wanted to spend every second with just my child since he had arrived.

I felt guilty when I thought I wasn't giving the other children enough attention, and I felt guilty when I gave the other kids attention, like I was somehow neglecting my own child. Even though my mom was my assistant with the day care, and helped me out with my own child as well, I just had this overwhelming gut feeling that I needed to just be with Joe. I could be up all night if I had to, and if it were just us, I could nap during the day when he did as well. I felt overwhelmed and tired, and I found myself crying in the mornings before the other kids came. I absolutely loved the other children, but it became just too much for me. I felt I hadn't taken enough time for just Joe and me. This was why I felt I had to give everyone a one-month notice and decided to close my day care.

The first year of motherhood was great. Joe was such a happy, silly boy. But since I had stopped the day care, it had put a financial toll on us.

I was doing a little bookkeeping for my mom's business, but Paul was still working 24-7, and everything was stretched so tight. We decided to sell the house and move farther down toward the Cape, about forty-five minutes away from our hometown. This would give Paul options for commuting to work, and we thought it would be nice to start fresh somewhere new. The new house wouldn't be ready for a few months, so we moved in with my in-laws for what was supposed to be a month or so but ended up being the whole summer.

I was a little bummed out that Joe's first birthday wasn't going to be in our first home, but my mother-in-law was very happy to open her home to all our friends and family. After all, our families had known each other since I was eight and my husband was thirteen; our brothers had grown up as great friends. His brother was even the best man at my brother's first wedding. Our moms had played softball together, and our dads had fished and gone boating together. It was a great birthday, a great day with some of our closest friends. Having kids all around who were the same age, we could see the next generation starting, and it was exciting. Joe was so cute, as he had started to walk; you know, that wobbly stage. A week or so later was Easter, and my sister-in-law loves to celebrate. She hung eggs from the trees and hid over two hundred eggs for an amazing Easter egg hunt. The cousins loved it! It was a great day, it was a great time in our lives, and we were so happy. Little did we know what was coming.

A few days later, Paul and I had to run some errands, and Joe stayed with his Grampa Nunzio and played with his cousins. The three of them were playing with a ball in the backyard. When we returned, my father-in-law told us that while Joe was playing, every once in a while, he would bend over, hold his stomach, and act like he was in pain. I was kind of dismissive of this. I had thought, *He's just a year old, and I don't think he would do that.* I thought my father-in-law had been overreacting or something. Until I saw Joe do it with my own eyes.

Over the next few days, Joe got worse. He was not feeling well and had diarrhea, severe stomach pains, and a high fever, and he was throwing up constantly. This was the first time he had ever been sick at all, besides having a runny nose from teething. We took him to the doctor, and they thought it was probably a bad stomach bug. They prescribed suppositories that were supposed to make the vomiting stop, but he just pooped them out. We had to get more, but they had to be specially made at the pharmacy. My mother-in-law and I were now driving around the South Shore trying to get more because the local pharmacy was out. It seemed that anything that could possibly go wrong did. However, at this point, we didn't even know the half of it.

By the second trip in three days to the doctor's office, the doctor said it was not just a stomach bug as he had initially thought, but something more serious. The doctor felt Joe's stomach and said, "You've got a really sick little boy here. You need to take him to the hospital right away." It was April 20, and our second anniversary, about two weeks after his first birthday.

One of the crazy things about this happening was that just weeks earlier, when I had Joe at the doctor for his one-year checkup, I watched another mom have the same thing happen to her. The doctor had appeared in the doorway and told her in a clear, stern, urgent voice that she needed to get her child over to the hospital right away. I remembered watching that mom and having a feeling of overwhelming sadness and fear for her, thinking, *Oh my God, how scary that must be.* I remembered sending her loving thoughts and prayers, thinking that, although I had no idea what was happening to her or her child, it could happen to any of us at any time. So, when I was having the same thing happen, it was like a déjà vu experience. It was very surreal.

Thankfully, the hospital was literally right next door. We got in the car and raced him over to the hospital where they were waiting for us. What happens next gets crazy and foggy. Everything was happening so fast, and we were extremely concerned, to say the least. The doctor there did reassure us that if it were something profoundly serious, he would send us directly to children's hospital in Boston. All I can remember is that they did some initial tests and took X-rays. I do vividly recall one test in which the nurses were trying to get a "clean catch" urine sample from our little baby. They had a bag with tape-like edges, and they pulled off the backing like on a Band-Aid and stuck it to the skin all around the baby's privates, so when he went, it went directly into the bag. There were three of them, two women and a man. I am not sure exactly what happened, but I think Joe may have started peeing, and he got pee on one of them or something, because they all started laughing hysterically, while Paul and I were crying and felt like we were about to physically get sick ourselves from seeing our child suffering in pain and confusion about what was going on. He was so young; he couldn't tell us how bad he was feeling.

We just looked at them like they had three heads each. But the nurses did this stuff every day, and looking back now, I can see how they would need some laughter in a job like that. However, currently and under the circumstances, it was not acceptable to us at all. We were beyond horrified at their behavior. I think they realized this because they saw us looking at them with disgust, and they stopped. Eventually, they let us know that they thought that it might be a burst appendix, but that is not common at such a young age. Not being 100 percent sure what it was, they were going to transport our son to Boston Children's Hospital because, no matter what it was, it was not good. A transport team from the children's hospital would bring him by ambulance, and my husband and I were told that we should go home and get some clothes and toiletries and meet them at the ER in Boston. We were like, "Um, excuse me?"

We were given specific instructions not to follow the ambulance and to not try to keep up with it because it could be dangerous. My husband and I had to leave Joe in the hands of strangers—doctors and nurses, yet strangers just the same. We were not allowed to go with them in the ambulance. I asked if I could ride in the front, and they said they didn't recommend it because it might be harder on everyone. I could not believe I was doing this. My poor baby only knew his parents, grandparents, aunts, uncles, and cousins. We were his whole world, and now we had to leave him with people we didn't know when he was so sick and all he wanted was his mom. It was one of the hardest things I have ever had to do. Somewhere in the back of my mind, I thought, *Well, they might want to separate the parent and the child to make sure there isn't some kind of abuse or something else going on.* I knew there wasn't, so I had to just trust them, and that's what we did. We called our parents and let them know what was going on and to meet us with some clothes and stuff at the ER in Boston. We may not have been able to go in the ambulance, but *hell no*, they couldn't tell us not to follow them. We raced after the ambulance the best we could, without causing any accidents.

We arrived at the ER at the children's hospital, and we found our baby being rocked in the loving arms of a warm and friendly nurse. She was a larger woman with beautiful, dark skin and an even bigger heart! She was so warm, friendly, and loving. I remember wondering on the way there about who would be with him and what he would do without me even for a second. When I saw this amazingly loving, warm, friendly woman talking to him, calming him, and swaying back and forth with my baby in her arms, a sense of relief and calm came over me. He wasn't even crying, at least not until he saw me, and then his little brain probably thought, *Oh yeah, that's my mommy!* She had been so calm and comforting and cozy to snuggle with, he most likely forgot about me. I so wished she could cradle me in her arms and tell me everything was going to be OK! Instead, she handed over my little lovebug, and I felt better holding him, smelling his hair and his sweet breath, and feeling his warm, little arms around my neck. God, I loved him so much, and I felt so helpless not to be able to fix whatever was wrong. Moms are supposed to be able to fix everything with a kiss, aren't they? Who would have thought our second anniversary could be worse than the first one? We cheered, with ginger ale and graham crackers, in an ER with our sick baby waiting for a doctor to come figure out what was wrong with him. Yup, this was definitely worse!

We waited for the on-call ultrasound doctor to get to the hospital because they still were not sure what was going on with Joe, but they were pretty sure it wasn't his appendix. We waited for what seemed like hours and hours. It was after midnight when we finally had the ultrasound done. This was not just an ultrasound tech performing it, it was the doctor! They'd called in the big guns. We did not know if we should be relieved or more worried. We were extremely thankful we had a doctor doing the test, while at the same time we could not stop wondering if it was because of the seriousness of the situation. And rightly so, this was a big concern!

The doctor took his time. He put the jelly-like cream on Joe's little tummy and went back and forth while looking at the monitor very carefully. The tests confirmed what he had suspected. Joe had what was called an intussusception, which is when the intestine telescopes up inside itself and causes a blockage. They are not 100 percent sure why this happens, but it can be the result of inflamed lymph nodes after an acute illness such as a viral bug. When they said this, I recalled when Joe had what we thought at the time was a cold, or possibly teething. We had gone to Connecticut for my nana's funeral, and we really didn't think much of it at the time. A little runny nose, maybe a slight temperature, but he was his typical, happy self. That's what a nonevent this teething or little cold had been. Nothing to even slow him down. But since he had not had so much as an earache until this point, I remembered it.

The doctor explained the options and what we (meaning *they*) were going to do. The first option, and the least invasive procedure, was to "blow" it out. Yes, this procedure works exactly as it sounds. They basically tape a large, straw-like tube to my child's bottom and blow air through it, trying to separate the blockage. Can you imagine? A one-year-old baby! But what choice did we have? We talked him through it the best we could, and we tried to keep him calm, while knowing he did not understand what the (bleep) was happening. They taped up his little bum, and on the third try, they almost had it. They kept upping the air pressure each time, but unfortunately, it wasn't working. Now they were afraid that if they tried with any more air pressure they could literally blow a hole in his intestine. Option one had not worked. On to option two: surgery.

It was now around 3:00 a.m. They had to do surgery. They would make a small incision and go into his belly, and hopefully, just pull the intestine, which should clear the blockage, and he'd be as good as new. However, there was a chance that his intestine could be damaged, and if this were the case, they might have to remove part of it, and he might have to have a colostomy bag. Then, once the inflamed intestine had time to heal, we would come back, and they would remove the colostomy bag and sew up his belly. For those who do not know, a colostomy bag is a bag that's attached to the outside of your body and holds your waste until the intestine can be put back into your body (where it belongs) to finish the "plumbing" necessary to have your waste come out where nature intended—not in a bag on the outside of your body!

They took Joe and got him ready as we were taken to a waiting room. I do not remember getting to watch him go under anesthesia or anything. We waited! They eventually came and got us. Time is not relevant in the hospital. Things either go way too fast or take an exceptionally long time. Nothing is as it should be. We got to see him in the recovery area, and they gave us the good news: no colostomy bag! The intestine looked red and raw but healthy enough to leave it.

The next time I interacted with my little boy, it was around six or seven in the morning. We were now on the surgery floor, and I was sleeping on one of those chairs that pull out into a makeshift bed in the same room as Joe, and my poor husband was asleep on a cot in the playroom somewhere down the hall. It was at this point that my baby Joe opened his beautiful, blue eyes, played peekaboo with me with "woobie" (which was his favorite blankie), was being silly with his Binky, and then quietly fell back asleep. Oh, how I would learn to treasure those simple, joyful moments of life.

In the days and weeks to come, my life as I knew it—and our life as a family—would be turned upside down, sideways, all around, and inside out. We would go to hell and back. His little body would go through unimaginable trauma that, even as an adult, is difficult to fathom. We would be tested over and over again. Our faith, our resolve, our human spirit, our love for each other and a higher power, our patience and kindness, all would be tested daily. And we would come to know the power of prayer from loved ones, our church family, and complete strangers. I would later look back at this time as the most difficult, but also the most spiritual, time in my life. I was not raised religiously, and somehow, in these emotional times, there was an inner power lifting us up. At our absolute lowest point, God, the universe, Spirit, a higher power—whatever you want to call it—was there to help us pick ourselves and each other up. When I was down, Paul would have some amazingly positive outlook or observation, and when he literally fell to the floor in tears of despair, I somehow came up with the words and the strength to pick him up and carry us both on.

The next morning, after we had gone back to sleep for a few hours, we were told we had to switch rooms. Somehow, Joe just wasn't himself; he was off. He would not really focus on you with his eyes, and he was making strange gestures with his hands. He was acting like he had an imaginary bottle, and he was drinking from it, even after he was just given a bottle. It was strange. I thought he was just asking for more because, at the time, he was only allowed a few ounces at a time because of the type of surgery he'd had. After belly surgery, he could not just suck down eight ounces of anything. But, unfortunately for Joe, he had already been switched to whole milk, and the doctors insisted on putting him back on a formula. I never understood this. I told them he was already drinking milk.

I asked, "What would you do if he was five? Would you put him back on formula? Can't we just try small amounts of milk?"

They said to me, "Well, he isn't five."

That was the most stupid answer I had ever heard. Instead, they kept trying to give him different flavored formulas in these little bottles, and he did not like them and would not drink them. They had put in so many different flavors and had tried to get him to drink them so many times that, once he was able to drink again, he would not touch anything in a bottle, and we had to give him milk out of the little individual cartons, like the ones from the school lunch, with a straw; that was the only way he would ever touch milk again. He did not trust anything in a bottle. That was not the way I had planned on weaning him off the bottle, but needless to say, he never touched a bottle again!

Sometimes I would get frustrated with him when he was motioning to drink from his imaginary bottle because I thought he was just being stubborn. What was actually happening at this time was that he was hallucinating. He was so thirsty that he was imagining a make-believe "bubba" and trying to quench his severely dehydrated and thirsty little body. But we did not know this at the time. I felt so bad for him, but I was exhausted from trying to explain to a thirteen-month-old that he had already had all the "bubba" the doctors would allow him to drink for now because his belly was tender. I knew he was hungry, but he would have to wait a little while longer before he could have more. He was constantly motioning and acting like he was drinking a pretend bottle. I was very tired and stressed and scared, and I didn't even know it at the time. We were just coping; we were in survival mode and thought we were doing OK.

A day later, some close friends and family members came to visit. I was excited for my nephew to come since he is Joe's favorite person in the whole world, and his big cousin by three years. Joe just adored him. His whole face would light up whenever he saw Brennan—usually. But to my dismay, when Brennan got there, Joe was still spacey. He would not, or could not, make and keep eye contact, even with his favorite cousin. We kept asking the attending doctors about Joe's bizarre behavior, but we were always told his vitals were fine, etc. Our family and friends had left, but my girlfriend realized she had forgotten her purse and had to come back and get it, and by then, she was in tears. Later, she revealed that she had been going through some personal stuff also, but that she just knew something was severely wrong with Joe at the time and she just could not handle it at all. I remember at the time thinking, *Gee, she's taken this really hard. He is going to be fine. Why is she so upset?* Apparently, I could not see the big picture.

You know when you are with someone every day, and you don't notice them growing and changing, but if you haven't seen them for a while, you notice they look different? I knew in my heart something was not right. I knew from that moment when Joe woke up and was not the same as he had been earlier when he was interacting with me. But the doctors kept telling us that he was fine. I think I wanted to believe them so badly that I almost just got used to Joe acting this way, but I still knew deep down that something just was not right. There was no interaction with him. He was there, you could say things to him, but his actions were not responses, they were just separate, unrelated noises or movements where previously he would respond and interact with you. Even though we were asking questions, the doctors kept giving us reasonable answers and justifying whatever we were questioning. I think I got frustrated with Joe's make-believe bottle routine because I could not do anything about it, and it was like he wasn't hearing me. I would ask him to stop, and he just kept on doing it, and I didn't understand—and neither did he. I always feel so bad when I think back to this time. No, of course, he did not understand why he could not have more to drink, but through his actions he was telling us something, and I just couldn't hear it or see it.

Eventually, our little twenty-pound baby swelled up and looked like an overinflated balloon. Our sweet, little thirteen-month-old baby boy's body had so much fluid, it did not know what to do with it. The human body is an amazing thing. We came to find out that when the body is stressed or is in distress, it sends fluid to the third zone, or outer layer. It is just under the skin and causes swelling. For example, after trauma like in childbirth, the mother will swell up in the face or ankles or all over. This is normal, and we recoup with proper rest and hydration. Well, Joe's little body was experiencing so much stress because it had become severely dehydrated that it was sending all the fluids to his third layer under the skin instead of to his organs.

He eventually started to turn red in the face and stiffen up, almost as if he were having a seizure, but then it would pass. At first it was like, "Am I seeing this right? Did he just do what I think I saw him do? Paul, do you see this? Did you notice what he just did?" It was so quick and sporadic and strange. But it kept happening, and there was no denying it, and we freaked out. It was not like a seizure; it was a seizure. I pressed that giant, red emergency button that's on the wall in the hospital room, and we screamed for the doctors to come, and they did, but the seizure had passed.

I said, "Just wait a second, it'll happen again! And look, we can't get him to follow my husband's finger with his eyes. He will not focus." The doctor on duty waited, and sure enough, it happened. Joe seized again. He decided to give Joe some medicine that was supposed to make him pee off whatever fluids he had been given. They were measuring every ounce of fluid that he drank, so they knew how much should come out. They gave it to him, and he had a catheter with a urine bag, and we watched as only drips came out. The father of the little girl in the bed next to us came over. He was a physician's assistant, and he told us that a whole lot more fluid should have come out into the bag, and it just was not right. Something was wrong, seriously wrong, and he knew it, too.

Before all this had happened, we had been up with Joe, trying to walk him around and get him moving again. The day before, the doctor had said we could probably go home over the weekend, and we were like, "Um, I do not think so! Do you see how swollen he is? Are you looking at the same kid?" He could not walk because his little body was so very swollen, but they did not realize that this just wasn't our kid. He did not look like Joe, and he wasn't acting like Joe; they did not know his normal body weight or his personality.

We were carrying him around the hall to get him out of his room, and we were talking. It was on this walk, the day before all the seizures started, that I told my husband I genuinely believed with all my being that something was wrong with his liver. I just had this overwhelming sense of knowing, but not knowing how I knew. I recalled a friend of a friend from when I was younger who had a liver issue, and she would swell up and look almost puffy. I couldn't remember whether it was from the treatment, the medicine, or just because her liver did not work properly. I just had this intuition that something was wrong with his liver. Why would I think of this person who I had met briefly at a beach house over twenty something years earlier? This memory just came to me out of the blue. I now believe that this memory was a message from Spirit, to give me knowledge of what was coming, or more accurately, what was already happening.

Thankfully, the dad of the little girl we were sharing a room with told us that this lack of urine was extremely bad, because we had no idea. And I think the young doctor was just as horrified but did not know what to say to us. The doctors then rushed Joe to the procedure room. He was still seizing and was crying badly. At the children's hospital, they have a policy not to do any procedures on the kids in their beds in the room, so they have a safe and comforting place where they know there are no owies, so all procedures are done in the procedure room. Plus, Joe was sharing a room, he was not in a single room.

I do not remember how he got there, or who picked him up and carried him there, but we were now in the procedure room. The doctors were trying to draw blood from his groin area, and he was crying relentlessly. The groin area is normally a particularly good place to draw blood from. The female doctor tried to draw blood as we comforted Joe and quieted him down, and she pulled back an empty syringe. There was a look of fright on her face. She tried it again, but still nothing. By the time she pulled back an empty syringe for the third time, a complete look of horror showed across not only her face but everyone's face in the room.

My husband and I did not know what all this meant, but it was exceedingly obvious to us that it was bad—incredibly bad. The doctors excused themselves for a minute. It was then that I noticed Joe had stopped crying! There was now only silence as my little precious, beautiful blue-eyed baby boy lay motionless and silent on the procedure table. I started praying for him to cry, where earlier I had begged for the crying to stop. All I could think was, *I didn't mean like this, God!* I just wanted him to feel better and stop crying so we could all focus, so the doctors could figure out what to do. *Not this quiet, Lord! Not like this! Not silence! Anything else …* *please, God! Not silence!* I begged.

After the female doctor had pulled back the empty syringe for the third time, I said to her, "No offense, but could you get the actual doctor, the head surgeon, to do this?" I tried to be polite, because I knew she was doing the best she could, but the other part of me was screaming, *This is my baby's life here. Come on, people, get it right the first time!* Because, of course, there was something wrong with the way she was doing it. There was blood in my baby! He was still alive, he was right there in front of me, and after all, they had been telling me for the past few days that his vitals were fine.

Thankfully, the head surgeon arrived in a flash. They asked our permission to try and take blood from a vein in our baby's head because, apparently, this is a good place to get blood from when someone is severely dehydrated and there is no other choice. No matter how dehydrated, no matter what, they should still be able to get blood from his head. I still do not think we realized the extreme severity of the situation and of this question that they were asking us until after it was over. Of course, we said yes. *Do whatever you have to; just please save our baby.* Doctor D., the head surgeon, put the needle into our thirteen-month-old baby boy's head very cautiously and slowly and gently pulled back on the syringe. There was blood! They ran from the room with it to try and figure out what the hell was going on. They thought he possibly could have intussuscepted again. They needed to rush him into an emergency surgery, but there were some complications.

So, once again, it was now somewhere around 3:00 a.m. I am convinced nothing good ever happens at 3:00 a.m. We called our families in again to be with us and support us. A nurse and a priest were also called to sit with us, and we were put in a small room with them. The nurse was telling me how beautiful my baby boy was, and all I could think of was, *How the hell do you know? You don't even know him. You have never seen him, seen who he is. Yes, he is beautiful, but what the heck do you know? You've only seen him with all that extra fluid on his tiny body. You do not know him. You do not know his personality. You have never seen his smile or heard his laughter. His laugh that is so big that his eyes are smiling back at you!* His eyes, he has the most beautiful, sky-blue eyes, just like my husband. My grandma once told my husband he had "bedroom eyes." He got so embarrassed, but that was just her way of saying he had beautiful eyes, and Joe had those same eyes. Would we ever get to see them shining up at us again?

I knew the nurse was just trying to be supportive and helpful, so thankfully, at the time, I just smiled at her and nodded when she said how beautiful my son was. I am sure my face must have had a look like, *Whatever, lady!* But I just smiled and looked at Paul like she was crazy. I have one of those faces that betrays my attempts to conceal my true thoughts and emotions. It's an "Oh, I'm sorry, did I roll my eyes out loud in your face?" kinda expression. Anyone who knows me knows this.

They rushed Joey to the MICU (multidisciplinary intensive care unit) and were trying to get him ready for another surgery. The doctors came and talked to us. He had gone into liver failure, kidney failure, and pancreatic failure, and they had no clue why. They needed to go back in and do another operation. They had to see if he had intussuscepted again, and they would possibly do a liver biopsy, but they needed to stabilize him first. They told us he may not make it. They were going to do everything they could, but we needed to be prepared. The hardest part was putting him under. He was so unstable that putting him under the anesthesia alone could kill him. We did the only thing we could: we said yes, and we put our faith in God and in the doctor's hands.

After what seemed like forever, the anesthesiologist, Doctor L., came and popped his head in. All I could think was, *What the heck are you doing here? Shouldn't you be in the operating room with my baby?* He quickly told us he just wanted to let us know that Joe had gone under the anesthesia fine. He was tolerating it, and he was doing good for now. We took a sigh of relief for a brief second and said thank you, knowing Joe was not out of the woods yet. But it was a win for the moment, and we would take it! Then the doctor ran back to the operating room. I can honestly say it was not until years later that I realized we had been put in the room with the nurse and the priest because they had thought Joe was going to die, or it was a pretty good chance that he was not going to make it. I know they said we had to be prepared, but how do you prepare for that? There is no way, and no amount of time could ever prepare you for your worst nightmare.

Well, Joe had made it back under the anesthesia, and no new intussusception was discovered, but since they had him there, they did a liver biopsy to see what was going on. The test showed his liver was only functioning at 30 percent, and toxins were going throughout his body.

We saw them wheel his bed back into the MICU. If I had not seen his doctors, I would not have known it was him. The child I saw was bloated to thirty pounds. That was ten tubes of fluid under the skin of a thirteen-month-old baby. He had tubes in his nose and his throat, he was on a ventilator, a machine was breathing for him, and he had monitors hooked up all over his body. My baby had become this unrecognizable, swollen creature on a breathing machine with blood on his face and tubes coming out from all over his body. There were beeps going off, and I could not handle it! For the first time since the whole ordeal had started, I had an anxiety attack and ran from the room. I thought, *That could not be my little baby boy lying there, it just couldn't be!*

I had cried before. I had felt hopeless. I had prayed constantly, in fact. I had never felt closer to God, or Spirit, but in that moment, I felt complete despair and disbelief. Nothing could have prepared me for what I saw; nothing could ever prepare a parent to see their child like that. The nurse came out and asked me what was going on. My child needed me, why had I ran from the room? I explained through heaves of hyperventilation and sobbing that his face was all bloody, and I could not handle it. They cleaned him up. I somehow calmed down and went back in to sit with my baby.

Joe went through many ups and downs over the next several weeks. He would take one step forward and two steps back. He was in a coma, he was in an isolation room in the MICU, and the family next to us had someone die. It was horrifying. We saw a family come in with a child who had meningitis and had just literally fallen to the ground at a birthday party. He got better and was moved to a different floor. We had to stay in a room for parents, with cots and curtains for walls. We were in this club that none of us had ever signed up for.

One morning, I found out the nurses had to change Joe's bedsheets, and my mom was in the room with him. She got to hold him, still hooked up to all those machines, but she got to hold him while they changed the sheets. I felt mad, jealous even. Why hadn't they come to get me? I was his mother! I was scared. What if I never got to hold him again? That's why I felt like that. I never said anything, and I was glad that, if anyone other than me got to hold him, it had been my mom. She had a special connection with Joe, maybe because he was my firstborn, maybe because she just loved him so very much. It's the connection every grandmother hopes to have with her grandchild, but somehow, she managed to make each of her grandchildren feel like they were her favorite. In all honesty, they all were her favorites. But at this time, it was just Brennan (the beloved older cousin) and Joe. No one else had been born yet. And she loved them both fiercely!

We would play music and read books to Joe all day, though we had no idea if he could hear us or not. He was still in a coma, although no one ever used that word. People sent us gift baskets with toys and books and notepads to keep a journal of questions that came up. One day, one of the doctors who had consulted on our son's case, and who was a world-renowned doctor, asked me if it was alright if he tape-recorded Joe crying. He was making a special for public television and needed recordings of kids crying. He was super nice, and I said it was OK, just as long as he didn't make him cry. If Joe was crying already, then sure, he could tape it. We had a nice conversation, and at one point he said to me, "You keep doing what you're doing! Playing music, reading to him, and talking to him! You never know, it could do even more good than the medicines we are giving him." This was mind-blowing to me at the time. I had previously believed that things were either science or religion. This was the first time I realized it could be both science and Spirit. It surprised me because I thought if you were a doctor, you were all science. It was comforting to know that this renowned doctor believed in Spirit, too! It made me feel that what we were doing was making a difference. And we know now that there have been many cases of recoveries from illnesses that prove that your mindset and how you feel have as much to do with your recovery as the medicine, if not more. A positive attitude and a hopeful spirit can make all the difference in the world. We were doing all we could, and we just could not do more than that.

I asked to give blood. I hated needles, but after seeing my baby go through all he had been through, I had no room to be scared of anything. Joe had been given multiple units of blood and platelets. He received it from donors who we will never know. They had saved his life with their generous, selfless donations. I felt that it was the least I could do. It was also something I could physically do. However, because of all the stress, I was down to 108 pounds. Apparently, once you are under 110 pounds, your blood is no good because they do not usually take it. I looked at them like, "Don't even tell me I can't do the one thing, the only thing, I can do!" I must have used my "Oh, sorry, did I roll my eyes out loud at you?" face again. Or they just felt bad for me because I was so pathetic. They agreed to take my blood. Who knows, they probably threw it away because it was too stressed out anyway. But they humored me, and at that moment, it was what I needed to do to feel useful in a situation I had no control of and where I was barely hanging on.

Joe had fevers that they could only get down with cooling blankets. Because of the damage done to his liver, which was only functioning at

30 percent at one point, they could not give him Tylenol. They had to put him on an experimental drug that is sometimes given to people who have overdosed on Tylenol, but it gave his body a rash, an allergic reaction they had warned us about. The rash spread all over his body, so they had to stop the medication. He got a few doses in before the side effects showed, so it could have helped, but there was no way of knowing for sure. His heart failed at one point. He had a rapid heart rate, and there was fluid around his heart. The toxins were making their way through his entire body. We prayed it would not go to his brain next.

He did continue to get better, and eventually, he even opened his eyes again. The first time Joe opened his beautiful blue eyes again, I was asking him where Brach was. Brach was our beloved chocolate lab. From that point on, I knew if he remembered Brach, he would remember us. I would not allow myself to think otherwise. The doctors were not so sure. Joe had actually already had toxins in his brain—that was why he'd had those seizures—and no one was certain what damage had been done. The only way to assess the damage was to wait and see how he reacted to mental and physical stimuli. They stuck feathers in his eyes to see if he would react, all kinds of crazy shit! I'd had enough one day when the "feather" doctors came around once again just as he had fallen asleep for his nap. I said, "*No! No more! Let him sleep. He needs rest to heal. If you must, come back when he's awake.*" You can do that; you can tell a doctor no!

One afternoon, all the nurses had been telling us to go home for a little while, and that they would watch over Joe. He was now out of the isolation room. Joe was still in the MICU but was doing much better. We reluctantly said OK, but I made sure I had someone from my family there. My brother had said he would stay with him, and then my dad showed up too. Paul needed a haircut desperately, and so we decided to go home for a few hours. We had been living with my in-laws while our new house was being built, so we headed there. When we got there, I felt this overwhelming feeling that we had made a big mistake. We'd had Joe's birthday party at their house only weeks before. His presents had all been opened but had not been played with very much. As we came into the house, our niece (my husband's sister's youngest daughter), who was only two months older than Joe, was playing with all Joe's toys.

I freaked out. I knew they did not mean anything intentionally, and normally I would never care if Ali were playing with Joe's toys. I would want him to share. He loved her and her sister, his older cousin Jenna. Joe's crib was in one of the bedrooms, and for some unknown reason, my mother-in-law found it necessary to store multiple pillows in his crib. Suddenly, I saw Ali playing with his toys, I noticed the pillows in his crib, and I felt like he should be there. *Damn it! He should be playing with his toys! He should be in his crib, not a bunch of pillows!* He was coming back, he was coming home, so why did it seem to me like they were not acting like he was coming home? Again, I was totally in a shocked state of mind. I had been traumatized by this whole ordeal and was looking at things from a completely skewed point of view. But I could not verbalize it, I couldn't say it. I did not even know how to begin to voice my feelings, and if I did, I didn't want anyone to feel bad because they were just living their lives. I think I realized life was going on while we were in the hospital, and I was afraid of it going on without Joe. I could not even fathom that idea! But they had no choice. They had to go on. They were not the ones with a sick child stuck in a hospital, not knowing if he'd ever come home again.

We flew back to the hospital. I made Paul cancel his hair appointment and take me straight back to my baby. To my relief, when we arrived, he was completely fine and was having fun with Uncle Bill and Grampy. A few weeks later, on Mother's Day, I got the best gift I would ever receive. We got to leave the MICU and go back down to the eighth floor, the surgery recovery floor. We spent a few more weeks recovering, and Joe kept making progress. He did a little physical therapy, and he had to crawl again before he could walk. But he just kept on progressing. And this time, when my brother brought his son Brennan to see Joe, Joe was ecstatic, and they both sat in Joe's hospital crib and blew bubbles! It was a beautiful day, and I can picture their smiles and hear their laughter in my memories as if it were yesterday.

That same day, Dr. L., the anesthesiologist, came to check on Joe, as all the doctors involved in Joe's case often did. He said something to us we will never forget. This was the man who had kept Joe alive during his second surgery when they thought the anesthesia alone could have killed him. On this visit to see Joe, Dr. L. let us know that he had never seen a child as sick as Joseph who had survived! And on the rare occasion a child had survived, while being almost as ill, they most certainly had residual ill side effects of some kind, some lasting damage. Joe, as far as we could tell at this point, had none! His words blew my mind.

One night, during Joe's stay in the MICU, my cousin (who lives in Connecticut) showed up. She and her husband had driven the three hours to come surprise us and give us moral support. She had asked to pray around his bed. The four of us held hands as she said a prayer. She spoke sternly to God. She told Him to send Joseph back to us with no ill side effects. She demanded it! It was amazing! This was at the time when he was still in a coma, and no one knew whether he would make it or not. And now Dr. L. was saying that it was almost a definite thing to expect a child as sick as Joe had been to have some type of ill side effect, whether it was mental or physical. But Joe had none! How was this possible? He had toxins flooding through every part of his body, he had multiple organ failures, and he was now perfectly normal! It was—and still is—a miracle.

He was a miracle child, a miracle story of survival. Was it the medicines, the doctors and nurses, the music playing, the read-a-louds, the love and cuddles from his Grammy, the support from friends and family members, the constant love from Paul and I, the love from "above," from Spirit? Just like the experimental drugs, we will never know for sure what worked and what did not, but I believe it was a little bit of all of it put together! He is living proof that there is power in prayer, and I will always be forever grateful to everyone for everything they did. From the skilled hands of his surgeons to our family members and friends, to the people I do not even know but knew someone who loved us and shared Joe's story. Whether it was a prayer, a conversation, a smile, or something greater, all of it contributed to Joseph and our family's healing. Although we will never be the same, I guess the residual side effect here is not something physical or mental, but possibly at the soul level. That residual side effect is to never take this life and this love for granted. And for that we are profoundly grateful and blessed!

Aerosmith's song, "I Don't Want to Miss a Thing," became my song to my baby Joe. I am so glad I didn't have to miss a thing! Once we were finally home, all I wanted was to stay in that moment with my baby, watching him sleep, kissing his eyes, and being so thankful he was still here. I would literally watch him sleeping, to make sure he was still breathing. I would love to see him chuckle in his sleep. It is so sweet to see a baby dreaming and smiling away and making those crazy, dreaming faces. For now, I just wanted to keep him with me, keep him safe, and never let him out of my sight ever again! I had also wondered where he had gone mentally when he had been in his coma, and I wondered if he had dreamed of me and his dad, and our dog, or if he spoke to Source or a relative who had transitioned, like how Harry Potter talks to Dumbledore after he had passed, and Harry dies briefly. Dumbledore told Harry it was his choice whether to go back or not. I wonder if Joe experienced something like this.

My favorite scene is when Harry asks, "Professor? Is this all real? Or is it just happening inside my head?"

Dumbledore responds, "Of course it's happening inside your head, Harry. Why should that mean that it's not real?"

This reminds me of the doctor telling me to keep playing music and reading and talking to Joe, because everything was real for him, only it was in his head. He was physically still there in that hospital bed, but mentally he was not there. This does not make where he was any less real than our physical environment. And it validates for me my belief in how powerful our thoughts are, not just in affecting but in creating our outer reality as well. "As above, so below, as within, so without, as the universe, so the soul …" Hermes Trismegistus, an ancient god, said that what we think and feel creates what we see and experience in our life circumstances. I will always wonder where Joe went in his head during his coma, and I will forever be grateful that he decided to come back home to us!

## CHAPTER 3

# The Diagnosis

· · · · · · · · · ·

We were allowed to leave the hospital on May 18, almost a full month since we had chased that ambulance, against the transport team's wishes, back on April 20, and a lifetime ago.

The doctors still did not have an answer as to why this had happened. They had told us a few theories and had taken a skin biopsy from Joe to test for some rare disorders, but it was highly unlikely he would have one because they are so rare. One of the theories was that a "toxic splash" had occurred. They thought perhaps when Joe's intestine was first pulled apart, some toxic intestinal fluid could have splashed out and sprayed on his other internal organs. But they just did not know for sure.

He was better now, he had stable vitals, and he was eating, drinking, playing, and smiling (except when he saw the doctors; then he would cry). But it was time; we could go home now. I was so nervous to take him home, scared that he would get sick again because we still did not know why this had happened. I had never been so nervous in my life. *What the hell should I do?!* I had my baby boy back, but I certainly was not the same person I had been a month ago! I was no longer blissfully ignorant. I was scared of everything. *What if he got sick or injured again? What do I do?* You never forget watching your child almost die, and it changes you.

We returned to my in-laws' house because our new house was still under construction. Joe was able to come back and play with all his birthday presents again. He had come home; somehow, those toxins had dissipated, and he came out of his coma, and was a "normal" healthy boy again. Except for the large scar across his abdomen, he was the same. The scar had started out about an inch or two long from the initial surgery, but now it went three-quarters of the way across his body. It was shocking to look at. We made up a funny story so Joe could have fun with it. He loved animals and had watched countless hours of nature shows about animals. As he got older, he would tell people his scar was from a shark bite. But he always knew we were being silly, and it was funny to see how people reacted.

When we were still at my in-laws', we started letting Joe sleep in our bed. Remember, I told you he was not a great sleeper, ever. Well, when he was sick in the hospital, my husband told him that if he pulled through this, he could sleep with us until he was eighteen, he did not care! It was one of those silly promises you make when you are desperate. Well, I honestly couldn't *not* have him next to me. I was so afraid he would stop breathing in the middle of the night. I would watch him lying next to me and I would literally watch him breathe. I would eventually fall asleep; exhaustion does that to you! He was now physically fine, but I was mentally fragile. The hardest thing about this was that we could remember and recall all of it. He, as a child, would forget, but we, as the parents, will remember forever.

After we moved into our new home, we finally got the call from the doctors. The skin biopsy they had taken from Joe's arm had come back. It was positive for one of those extremely rare diseases, a metabolic disorder. It was called a fatty oxidation disorder, or FOD for short. It was a sad and scary moment, but it was also a relief because it explained a lot about what had happened to Joe. This diagnosis would give us much-anticipated answers, or so we thought. The reason Joe had gone into multiple organ failure was that, when his body ran out of energy, it went to his fat or "food stores," but because he lacks the proper enzyme to break down fat and turn it into energy, it caused a toxic effect, and those toxins then went throughout his entire body.

It only takes a child four to six hours without an outside energy source to supply energy for his body before his body will go to his food stores, and in Joe's case he hadn't been able to keep anything down for about forty-eight hours before he had been brought to the hospital. When he was in the hospital, he was given IV fluids but not at the proper dextrose level for a child with an FOD. That IV is what kept him alive, but at the same time, it was not enough sugar or dextrose, and that was why he kept getting sicker but stayed alive. He was allowed only a minimal amount of oral liquids because of the type of surgery he had gone through, and it was almost a week after he first got sick that they took him off the IV completely. That was when he spiraled down and started having the seizures. A person with an FOD needs a 10-percent dextrose level in his or her IV; the standard amount given is 5 percent. Joe was getting half the amount he needed.

They do have newborn screenings to test for a number of these rare disorders. That is when they prick a little spot on your child's heel at birth. It does depend on which state you are born in; not all states do all the tests. Also, depending on the year you were born, not all tests were mandated, even if they did do some in your state. Once you know that someone has one of these disorders, then you can take extra precautions if that person is ill, like with a stomach bug or flu or when a surgery is needed. Any time a person with an FOD has to fast or cannot get external energy sources into their body, they need to have this high dextrose level of IV fluids. In Joe's case, he needs 10 percent dextrose IV plus electrolytes if he is continually vomiting, has severe diarrhea, must have surgery, or if for any reason he is not eating or cannot eat. He must be allowed to eat or drink every four hours during the day, but he can sleep through the night without having to be woken up to eat. There are many different types of FOD. It is believed that Joe has what is called a long-chain transporter defect. This was only determined after a specific diagnosis was unable to be determined.

How did Joe get this? Apparently, we hit the jackpot! This disorder is autosomal recessive, meaning my husband and I both have the same bad recessive gene. When a child is created, he gets one gene from his mom and one from his dad for every characteristic. The parents each have two to pick from for every gene in the new life. There are genes for everything from eye color to height to internal organ structures, and every other characteristic of the new human body being created. So, for example, if Mom has a good and a bad gene, and Dad has a good and a bad gene, you can get any combination of these.

In the example below, Mom's are MG (mom good) and MB (mom

bad), and Dad's are DG (dad good) and DB (dad bad), so you can get any of these combinations:

- MG & DG – both good
- MG & DB – one good/one bad (a carrier)
- MB & DG – one bad/one good (a carrier)
- MB & DB – both bad

The good gene takes over if there is one bad and one good, so you are still OK, but you are a carrier of the disorder and may give it to an offspring if you marry someone who is also a carrier. But when both genes are bad, that is when there is an issue.

Let me backtrack a little, just to make sure you understand how rare this is. The doctors let us know that it is a one in a million chance that you will meet someone else in your lifetime who has the same bad gene as you. Paul and I have known each other since we were kids, and then we grew up and got married. We have known someone with the same bad recessive gene our whole lives, and then we got married. The odds are one in a million to meet, and we got married and had a child! If you have done the math from above, the odds were astronomical that we met and got married. And if you consider my above examples, you will understand that each of our children will now have a one in four chance of having this metabolic disorder. Although the disorder would be the same in any child, each child could handle it differently. Just as each individual person handles a cold differently, has allergies or not, has a queasy stomach or a rock gut, it all depends on each child's constitution. This is what will determine how their body handles the disorder. But since we now know about it, we can handle or manage it beforehand. No other child of ours should ever get this sick again.

Joe's FOD is unspecified, meaning they know he has one, but they are not sure which exact one. Back when he was diagnosed, there were thirty to forty known metabolic disorders. Over the years, this number has increased as they have identified more. To this day, Joe's is still unspecified. We wondered how we would have more kids. Is it selfish, or is it selfish not to? What about Joe? We never envisioned having an only child. We loved our siblings and could not imagine our lives without them, and we always said we would like to have three or four kids. There are lots of only children in the world, but that is just not what we had envisioned. Were we going to let this diagnosis scare us into not having more children out of fear? What was the responsible thing to do? Responsible for society, responsible for Joe, responsible for any future child? And what if those were different things? *What do we do?* It is not something you can answer right away. We decided we would have to do some research and soul-searching to decide for ourselves what was right for us.

In hindsight, I realize I was definitely in a deep depression once we were home, and even more so once we moved into our new house. I loved my son so much. Why was I sad all the time? Why didn't I have the motivation to do anything? We would spend our days watching Disney movies, going to Ocean State Job Lot, and playing outside with our dog, Brach. I would be watching a movie and thinking, *What if this is the last time I ever see this movie? Because I could die. Anyone could die at any moment.* I had Joe home, and he was alive, so why was I so depressed and scared? I eventually came to believe that it was because I was mourning the loss of the child I thought I was supposed to have. One who did not have an FOD, one who was "healthy" in every sense of the word, not just on the outside. But he was alive, and I knew how blessed and fortunate we were to have him still on this earth with us. So what the hell was wrong with me?

I had been in a car accident in high school. It was a pretty bad one, but I came out of it with only a few bumps and bruises, and it was determined to be 100 percent the other driver's fault. I would think so, since her license plate ended up embedded in my radiator, and she was on the wrong side of the road because she thought she was on a one-way street. I went through days of extreme lows and then days of extreme highs after this happened. I was eventually diagnosed with post-traumatic stress disorder (PTSD). I had PTSD because I had never been in a life-or-death situation before, and it scared the shit out of me. I even felt suicidal for a brief time. I recall thinking that, if I could not control whether I lived or died, I would control how and when because I wanted control of my life. I quickly realized that I was not able to harm myself in any way. And I now know this was all about feeling a lack of control, and that when you feel like you have no control over your own life, you can go to a very dark place. After Joe's experience,

I think I was again in another very dark place, with a lack of control but an understanding of the emotions having gone through these feelings before.

During this time, I came across an essay that caused me to reevaluate things. It is about having a disabled child. Joe's disability is on the inside. He looks like a "normal" kid, he has "normal" intelligence, but he is not "normal" on the inside. I think of the FOD as an ugly monster that rears its head when the body is in a crisis. It lies dormant in everyday life, you may even forget it is there, but if you are ill or when your defenses are down, it comes after you with a vengeance. I also was not "normal," and I had seen horrible things. I had gone through an emotional tsunami. Now I was on the other side of it, but somehow, I was still feeling the pain from it, all while knowing I did not want to be sad and scared anymore. The essay is titled "Welcome to Holland," and it is about loving where you are at, even if it was not where you had planned to be.

"Welcome to Holland"
Emily Perl Kingsley

I am often asked to describe the experience of raising a child with a disability - to try to help people who have not shared that unique experience to understand it, to imagine how it would feel. It's like this … …

When you're going to have a baby, it's like planning a fabulous vacation trip - to Italy. You buy a bunch of guide books and make your wonderful plans. The Coliseum. The Michelangelo David. The gondolas in Venice. You may learn some handy phrases in Italian. It's all very exciting.

After months of eager anticipation, the day finally arrives. You pack your bags and off you go. Several hours later, the plane lands. The flight attendant comes in and says, "Welcome to Holland."

"Holland?!?" you say. "What do you mean Holland?? I signed up for Italy! I'm supposed to be in Italy. All my life I've dreamed of going to Italy."

But there's been a change in the flight plan. They've landed in Holland and there you must stay.

The important thing is that they haven't taken you to a horrible, disgusting, filthy place, full of pestilence, famine and disease. It's just a different place.

So you must go out and buy new guide books. And you must learn a whole new language. And you will meet a whole new group of people you would never have met.

It's just a different place. It's slower-paced than Italy, less flashy than Italy. But after you've been there for a while and you catch your breath, you look around. … and you begin to notice that Holland has windmills … and Holland has tulips. Holland even has Rembrandts.

But everyone you know is busy coming and going from Italy … and they're all bragging about what a wonderful time they had there. And for the rest of your life, you will say "Yes, that's where I was supposed to go. That's what I had planned."

And the pain of that will never, ever, ever, ever go away … because the loss of that dream is a very very significant loss.

But … if you spend your life mourning the fact that you didn't get to Italy, you may never be free to enjoy the very special, the very lovely things … about Holland.

This essay made me realize that there was nothing wrong with me. I didn't have to mourn losing the "healthy" child I had always thought I'd have; I could be thankful that he was here, and that I was here, and that my husband was here, and we could stop caring about what had been lost and start embracing what we had. We could go to Holland, and it could be a beautiful journey. It was all going to be OK.

I joined an FOD support group and helped other families go through their beginnings of being diagnosed, and it helped me to help others. Eventually, I stopped because I just could not have my life be about the most horrible experience of my life. I am very emotional, and I just could not detach enough. I needed to be happy, to enjoy my life with my husband and my son. So, for myself, I had to step away from the support group, and I just hoped that I had done some good for those who I had interacted with during that time. I commend those who do this type of work, because it is so needed, but it was time for me to move on. Maybe it was time now to start thinking about having more children.

---- CHAPTER 4 ----

# *What the Heck Is a Blighted Ovum?*

· · · · · · · · · ·

We had come home from a recent trip to Florida. The trip had been planned before Joe had gotten sick. In fact, if he had gotten sick one week later, he may not have lived. Had we been in Florida, instead of at home where we were so close to Boston and so fortunate to get to go to Boston Children's Hospital, the number one pediatric hospital in the world, I highly doubt he would be here, and I would be telling a completely different story. So now we decided it was time for a much-needed getaway. We had fun, and Paul got to see his biological father. I was overly cautious with Joe, but for good reason. When Paul Sr. decided to play rough with him in our hotel room, tossing him around on the bed, I almost lost my shit! Paul Sr. was a rough-and-tumble kind of person, but now I wanted to scoop up my precious, fragile baby, wrap him in my arms, and tuck us away where nothing would ever happen to him again. Sort of like in the movie *Finding Nemo*.

*Finding Nemo* is my husband's favorite kid's movie! We have watched it many times. The story is actually pretty horrifying. The story goes that Marlin, the dad clown fish, loses his wife and all but one of their offspring to a vicious fish who attacks and eats them. After he rescues and raises the only surviving egg (his son, Nemo), they realize Nemo has one "lucky" little fin and one regular-size fin. Marlin is very overprotective of Nemo because of his "lucky" fin, and Marlin subconsciously believes it holds Nemo back in certain ways. Nemo goes to the Drop Off where their reef meets the big ocean, upset because his dad does not think he can do what all the other little fish can do, just because of his "lucky" fin. He swims out to a boat and ends up getting taken by a diver.

As a parent, this is a most horrifying idea. First you lose your spouse, then shortly after, someone steals your only child, your son! And to top it off, Marlin had promised Nemo nothing bad would ever happen to him. Once Marlin meets Dory and tells her this story, she finds it strange. Why would Marlin promise that nothing would ever happen to Nemo, ever? Dory does not understand because she thinks it would be so boring if nothing ever happened to Nemo. It makes me think of how I felt after we first came home from the hospital with Joe after his illness. I did not want anything to happen to him. I wanted to protect him and shelter him from anything and everything, not because I did not believe in him, but because I had seen bad things in life. I had seen and felt horrible things, and I never wanted to do that again, and I never wanted him to have to go through anything bad ever again!

So, from this seemingly horrible situation in which Nemo is taken, Marlin, although frightened himself, learns to live from love. His love of his son outweighs his fears of the unknown, and he sets out on an amazing adventure, conquers his fears, meets characters he had only dreamed about, and is motivated by his love and desire to find and reunite with his son. So many things happen to all of them, and from these incidents, they grow and become more fully who they were meant to be. Nothing changes in Marlin except his thoughts. This does not mean he was never frightened or scared, but he pressed on and moved through his fears and came out the other side stronger and more fulfilled and fully living, being the best version of himself, the one he was meant to be.

I could shelter Joe, but he would never get to learn and grow. I could keep him safe and away from harm, but he would not get to ever believe in himself. I had to learn to live from love, or he would end up resenting me. I had to let my love for my son outweigh my fears of what could go wrong. It was time for me to start trusting and learn to focus on the positives, because they far outweighed the negatives.

We can all take a huge life lesson from this amazing Disney movie! Living from love not from fear, I can live a life full of amazing adventure and love, even beyond my wildest dreams! I realized I was being like Marlin in that moment, not wanting anything to ever happen to Joe. But then life would be so boring. I never wanted anything bad to happen to Joe, but what about the life lessons that come from seemingly difficult times? Don't they help us build character and depth of spirit? How do I protect him and allow him to follow his own heart's desires? It was extremely hard to not wrap him in Bubble Wrap and tuck him away somewhere where he would be safe. I thought the boy in the bubble had it all figured out. Ha ha! I would have to learn to live from love, and not from fear, which would prove to be one of my life's biggest challenges and blessings. Because, without that ability, I would not have gotten much farther along my life's journey.

It was about a week after coming back from our trip to Florida, and I still had left the suitcases out on the floor with the laundry in them. We were now living in our new home; however, it was about forty-five minutes away from our hometown. We felt we wanted to move back. We missed the support of our friends and family, and we realized through such a difficult time that we really did want to be close to them and wanted to stay in our hometown. Being home with my son, I was always nervous, and now I was away from family and friends too! It was not a good situation for my mental health, either. We had a great support system, but it was now forty-five minutes away, and it was hard to not be able to just have my mom two minutes down the road like before, especially now that we were pregnant again! I still do not know exactly how we came to the decision to have more children, except that I always thought I'd like my kids to be about two to two and a half years apart, and my loving husband, as usual, agreed with me.

It wasn't long before we realized just how much we'd need our families again. I don't remember what day of the week it was, just that it was incredibly early in the morning. I woke up with an uncomfortable feeling. It was like I had wet my pants, or like the feeling when your period overflows and leaks past your pad and onto your underwear and sheets. Everything felt damp and heavy. I got up and walked through the dark into our bathroom. I put the light on and sat on the toilet. My pajama bottoms were soaked in blood. It was everywhere. There was dark red blood all over me, like I had been stabbed. I called to Paul. I was in shock. The bleeding would not stop. He called my doctor and my mother. We woke up baby Joe and planned to meet them both at the hospital in forty-five minutes. We rushed as fast as we could, safely driving the forty-five-plus minutes to the hospital where my doctor was. My mom was waiting in the lobby of the ER, and she took Joe and gave me a kiss. My doctor came, and she said I would have to have a dilation and curettage (D&C), so Paul went back with my mom and Joe to wait in the waiting room.

After the procedure, my doctor said it had all gone well. A D&C, for those who do not know, is a procedure in which they dilate your cervix so they can scrape the uterine lining to remove abnormal tissue with a spoon-shaped instrument called a curette. My doctor said my pregnancy was what they called a blighted ovum. This occurs when a fertilized egg implants in the uterus but does not develop into an embryo. Your body thinks it is pregnant, and it is producing all the hormones; however, there is no developing fetus in the embryonic sac, and therefore, no baby. I had just experienced my first miscarriage. Apparently, these are fairly common, but I had never heard of this before, and I was quite devastated.

Was this a sign that we should not have more kids? Were there other genetic issues besides the metabolic disorder coming into play? Was there something wrong with me? There were so many questions. Most of all, would we still be able to have more children, or was this decision being made for us? Would we consider adoption? Or would Joe be an only child? We did not have the answers. Only time would tell. All we could do at this point was to be thankful for each other, and our baby Joe, and our families. We knew for sure now that we wanted and needed to sell the house and move back home as soon as we could.

As if the story could not get screwier, we already had the house on the market, and our real estate agent tried to contact us while we were gone at the hospital for the day. When we got home, we received a message that the agent had actually shown our house while we had been gone for the day. She had tried to call, but she got our voicemail and just went ahead and showed the house anyway without hearing back from us. The house with our suitcases full of laundry and a murder scene in our master bathroom. How lovely! *Are you f—ing kidding me? WTF?* She was promptly fired. We sold the house with a new agent, and we moved back home within the next few months. We were so glad to be back home!

It felt like a fresh start. It was the beginning of April and the start of spring. Shortly after moving back home, it was also Joe's third birthday. I was mentally in a much better place. I had decided to do whatever I could to help my chances of conceiving again. I read information about eating organic foods and doing yoga. I changed many habits, eating only organic foods, then only organic warm foods. I did fertility yoga, and I stopped drinking alcohol. I also started a daily ritual of drinking a shot of wheatgrass juice. I had read about it in a couple of books, and I figured if it could help my fertility, then *bottoms up*!

I do not know if you have ever tasted wheatgrass juice before, but you'd definitely remember if you had. It is a distinct flavor of grass. It literally tastes like someone took grass clippings from the lawn mower and mushed them up with a little water in a blender but left it slightly chunky. It was expensive, too, and I had to buy it at the organic food store. I tried it in a mix, but then I would have to make an eight-ounce glass of it. I ended up opting for the one-ounce frozen concentrate. I would just put it in warm water to defrost it, leaving it in its container, and after a few minutes, I would pop off the cover and shoot it down the back of my throat. I was gonna be the healthiest version of myself that I had ever been.

Before I knew it, it was the holiday season. Thanksgiving was always my mom's favorite! This year, I had exciting news that would make her day even more happy. I was pregnant again! Christmas was right around the corner. What a fun time the holidays are when there is a little one in the family. Joe was extremely excited for Christmas. Unfortunately, a few days before Christmas, I started to bleed. It was not like before; it was spottier. I still did not feel good about it. I went to the doctor, and they confirmed my numbers were going down, not up, which meant I was having another miscarriage. I remember just being so sad.

On Christmas morning, with my mom by my side, I had my blood taken to confirm my body was losing the pregnancy on its own and I did not need another D&C. I recall talking with my brother, and he said, "Try to stay upbeat and positive for Joe!" He was right, but sometimes, no matter how hard you try, you just cannot deny how you are truly feeling, especially when your hormones are crashing in on you like a wave of emotions filled with sadness, melancholy, and just *blah*. But I did it. I put on a happy face and smiled because my son deserved a happy Mom for Christmas. I could be sad on another day.

I had made the mistake many do, by telling my family and my son that I was pregnant. I had just been so excited, and I wanted to tell everyone and did not want to think about the possibility of anything going wrong again. Maybe I thought if I told everyone then it would have to be OK? I now had to deal with the reality that I was no longer pregnant. I also had to explain to Joe that he was not going to have a brother or sister. And I realized, through the mouths of babes, as they say, how this affected not only myself but our families. I had taken my nephew Brennan and Joe to the park one day. As I was pushing them on the swings, another woman and her child had come up next to us, and we realized they were looking for something. We started chatting with them and asked if we could help them find what they were looking for. To my horror, Brennan announced matter-of-factly to this complete stranger, "Yeah, my auntie lost her baby!" He did not understand, and he actually thought I had lost—as in misplaced—my baby, like these people had lost something, and thought I could not find it. She looked at me with sympathy and pity. I shrugged my shoulders and nodded yes. He was not wrong; I had lost my baby. Perhaps, this was the day I could be sad.

## CHAPTER 5

# *They Don't Know What the (Bleep) They Are Doing!*

· · · · · · · · · ·

Now that I'd had two miscarriages, my ob-gyn thought it would be a good idea to see the fertility doctors. In January they met with me and decided to put me on Clomid. Clomid is the fertility doctor's first line of defense. It is a drug that is supposed to help you ovulate and conceive. The following month, they did blood tests and said it did not look like I was ovulating at all. This made no sense to me since I had been using ovulation predictor kits for months and always got a positive result. These doctors were very sterile in their interactions with me. They seemed like they were very matter-of-fact and not very personable. I did not get a good feeling from the start when I met them. Now they were saying I was not ovulating? *WTF! They are crazy!* I thought, *They do not know what the heck they are talking about. They don't know what the (bleep) they are doing!*

I decided to stop going to them. Instead, I chose to follow my gut, and to look for answers that resonated with me. I began to follow a system in a book about fertility. It helped create awareness of what your body is feeling and what signs to look for to know what phase of your cycle your body is going through. I had always had fairly regular cycles, usually twenty-eight to thirty days and very predictable, and it just so happened I was just about to end one cycle and start a new one. Perfect timing! Even though the book was designed to be read first, following along the first month and then learning what to do in subsequent months, I just dove right in.

The book said to follow it for a couple of months to learn to tune into your body and to be able to truly understand what part of your cycle you are at and the signs that distinguish one phase from the next. Like I said, it was perfect timing because my period had started a day or so before, and I understood and figured out these concepts right off the bat. We followed what the book said for when the best time was to conceive. Usually, a day or two after the end of your period is best, but other factors can also affect that. For example, if you stay up late or drink alcohol, then your temperature could be off the next day, and it can be hard to identify accurately. The basic basal temperature upon waking at the same time every day, put together with physical signs, gives you the picture of your menstrual cycle's stage. I started charting my cycle on day four of my cycle, March 7. All the physical signs were there that I was indeed ovulating, and we took advantage of the best days to conceive according to the book. On the twenty-eighth day of my cycle, March 31, I had a positive home pregnancy test result.

I went to my doctor's office two days later, and a positive blood pregnancy test confirmed that I was indeed pregnant! Because of the previous miscarriages being early on, it was thought I may have a progesterone deficiency. Even though the progesterone levels were good for the moment, they still started me on Crinone (at 8 percent), a progesterone supplement used when the indication of a progesterone deficiency is suggested. My morning temperatures remained high, and my boobs ached, both good indications of a healthy pregnancy. However, on the eight-week mark, approximately the same time it had happened in the last pregnancy, I started spotting. This time, I did not have any cramps. The spotting was light for the day, and I just kept reminding myself that spotting around this time can also be from implantation. Around this time, the embryo burrows into the uterine wall. This is called implantation. By the next day, the spotting stopped. I was indeed pregnant again! I now believed I did not have secondary infertility or an ovulation problem as the doctors had suggested. Joe was not going to be an only child! This time, I would wait to tell him and the rest of the family, but I had a good feeling about this pregnancy.

Now other concerns began. Would this child have the same metabolic disorder as Joe? How would we be sure? How could we keep this baby safe?

Through our metabolic doctor collaborating with my ob-gyn's office, they came up with a plan. Since whatever Joe had did not show up on newborn screens, they would take a sample from the umbilical cord at birth and send it off to the lab for testing. This way, they could test the cells without having to do a skin biopsy on a newborn. We had specific instructions for the delivering doctor on how to obtain the sample and put it in a test tube on ice, and how and where to ship it. It was amazing. And this child would still get whichever newborn screens are done in Massachusetts, as well. Once we had this plan in place, it was a bit of a comfort.

I was still nervous for many reasons. I was no longer blissfully ignorant! But because I was no longer so naive, I offered to take part in a study. This meant I got extra ultrasounds, which meant extra opportunities to see how my baby was doing. The study was measuring the baby's femur to see how it correlated to certain birth abnormalities such as Down syndrome or dwarfism. Again, it felt good to help others. If the information from my pregnancy could help other people, and it was noninvasive, and I got extra peeks at my unborn child, then it was a win-win in my book.

We found out we were having another boy. We were all extremely excited! I was glad he and Joe would have each other, and if he did have the metabolic disorder too, I thought it could be something they would be able to help each other with. I liked the idea of having two boys; best buds, best friends, and now since they would be almost five years apart, I thought it would help keep them close that they were both going to be boys.

At the time, we liked to watch the TV show *Survivor*. We were also trying to decide on a baby name, and Joe thought Colby, because of the guy who won *Survivor*. We all liked it, and then Joe came up with his middle name too. He had a friend at church named Jim. This was the church where Joe had been baptized, and the same people who had prayed for Joe when he had been so sick. These were very dear and special people to us. There was always a special bond between Joe and Jim. He was easily the oldest parishioner in the church, and Joe was one of the youngest, but they would strike up conversations. God only knows what they were talking about, but they had an unmistakable bond. Jim had recently passed away. Joe was not so sad about it at the time, even though he was little. He would sometimes howl like a wolf in the car and say that was how he was talking to Jim now. I figured Jim's spirit had come to him as a wolf in a dream or something. Anyway, Joe said he wanted his baby brother's middle name to be for his friend, and wolf-spirit, Jim, so Colby James it was.

As the pregnancy progressed, I was enormous! I am only five feet four inches tall, and only because I lie and add a quarter of an inch because it's easier to say. I actually gained less weight than with my first full-term pregnancy (with Joe). But my stomach was like another appendage. It looked like you could have taken it off of me and set it next to me like a giant beach ball! I could not believe I weighed less, albeit only a few pounds, but still less. The year Colby was born, Thanksgiving was on Thursday, November 22. It was awfully close to my due date, and I thought I might go into labor. I think I ate everything in sight to try to induce labor. It was a long few days. I thought I felt contractions, so they put me on a monitor to check, but then they said they really did not think it was time yet.

My doctor set a date for inducing my labor, and it was the next day. The doctors on duty at the hospital were questioning me about why I was scheduled to be induced, and I was just like, "Do you not see the size of me?" In truth, I honestly was not sure why, except that my doctor kept saying Colby was most likely going to be a big baby. Joe had been seven pounds nine ounces, and the doctor kept telling me at checkups that Colby was going to be a bigger baby. When I would ask how much bigger, she purposely would not give me a straight answer. Once the covering doctor from my OB's office came on, he decided that, given these factors, along with wanting to have a doctor who knew about the metabolic protocol and umbilical collection, they decided to keep me and let me labor.

Believe it or not, I cannot remember if they gave me any Pitocin, but if they did, it was not nearly like before. What I do remember is getting to a point during the contractions where it hurt so badly that I was holding my breath. Once I realized I was doing this, I said to my husband that, although I did not want to have an epidural, maybe it was time to consider getting one. Even though I was doing my best to breathe through the contractions, I was concerned that holding my breath during the pain was not good for the baby or myself. I knew I needed to breathe for myself and my baby, and I did not want to do anything to jeopardize his health.

We mentioned this to the nurse after the last contraction subsided. She said that it unfortunately looked like it was too late, and I was going to have the baby very shortly. It would be a painful but quick experience. I said, "OK, I can deal with that!" The doctor came in the room with a mouthful of lunch, still chewing, with his face shield on. Once Colby decided it was time, he came fast and furiously. The doctor did ask if he could do an episiotomy, since I had torn so much from Mr. High-Five (a.k.a. Joe). I said yes because I now knew it would be easier to stitch and heal this way. When he came out, he was like a human cannonball. Colby was gigantic.

Colby James was born at nine pounds twelve ounces, and he was twenty-two inches long. Um, yeah, I would say that is a little bigger than Joe. Holy guacamole! He was over two pounds heavier and three quarters of an inch longer. Remember, I am only five feet four inches tall, and I weighed about 120 pounds at the start of every pregnancy. Joe was the first person to get to hold him. He was so excited! Joe was also starting to catch a cold on the day we were to go home. Now I was nervous again. I had nursed Colby the entire time in the hospital. When I had nursed Joe, I'd had an issue with milk production, so I wanted to make sure I was doing everything I could to promote it this time. I did not want bottle supplements in the hospital because I was concerned it could interfere with my milk production for this baby. He was doing great. I was exhausted, but that's par for the course. He was beautiful, and the nurses said it looked like he had frosted tips in his hair, which was noticeably lighter on the ends. Joe had had a full head of dark hair that had fallen out in clumps before growing back. My two boys were different in many ways, but also similar in their features. They both had little button noses, fair complexions, and symmetrical features, and Colby had blue eyes too! Another miracle baby, a rainbow baby, though I did not know that term then. He was the joy we had been hoping for!

When Colby was a few months old, we still did not have any answers from the umbilical cord tests that had been sent out right after he was born. Being so large, he wanted to start sleeping through the night. Our metabolic doctor wanted him fed around the clock because a baby cannot go as long without food as an older child. One night, I was trying to wake him up to nurse, and he wanted nothing to do with it. I had to strip him down naked and make him cold, trying to wake him up. I put cool washcloths on him. It was awful. I felt like I was torturing him. After that, I decided, if we had to measure how much Colby was drinking, I would have to be up to pump and put it in a bottle to measure it. There was no other concrete way to measure how much he was getting when nursing, so I might as well start some formula. I was not against formula; I just wanted to give my child the best start and thought that was by nursing. I still do, but I also know there is nothing wrong with formula, and it is also some people's choice to never nurse. To each their own. At this time, formula was what would work best for all of us. It had been a couple months, he had gotten all the colostrum and benefits from nursing, and now I needed the benefits of someone else—a.k.a. Daddy—to be able to feed him so I could get some rest. Also, this came with a lot less worrying. We could say exactly how much he drank, and we could let him sleep without worrying because we could see how much he'd had before he had gone to bed, and then we could gauge when he would need more food.

A short time later, the doctors confirmed Colby also had an FOD. I remember crying, feeling like it was so crazy, and feeling a little guilty that he would also have this burden to bear. He would now have a "special belly" too. The big difference was that now we knew from birth, so if there was ever a need, we could take precautions to ensure his safety. Eventually, it just became part of what we had to do if they got ill. In our everyday life, it was not much of a factor. I would always have snacks on me when we went anywhere for any amount of time. We ate regular meals and had tons of snacks. Colby was always a good eater. The only times when this was difficult were if we had a busy day, because he was also always a good sleeper. If he were to fall asleep before he had dinner, I would have to wake him and get him to eat. Because he was such a good sleeper, this proved difficult at times, especially on one family vacation when we could not get into a restaurant to eat early enough. There were times when he would fall asleep with his head in a plate of food. It was funny, and I learned to give him snacks, especially when we could not control the time frame for when we were going to be able to eat. We all learned to handle it and do the best we could. For the most part, Joe and Colby did awesome.

A stomach bug was the one thing that would definitely send us to the hospital. Once, when Joe was young and Colby was still a baby, Joe got a stomach bug. Paul and I took him to the hospital. The three of us had been in a cubical in the ER for hours together before Paul left. I was staying in a room with Joe because he had to have IVs overnight, when

I started vomiting in the hospital room bathroom. Paul called me when he arrived home to relieve the grandparents from babysitting to say the baby was fine, but he'd had to pull over on the highway to vomit on his way home. Thankfully, baby Colby never got sick. I think his immune system must have still been super strong. Over the years, what we had to do became routine, and it never outweighed the joys of life with my two beautiful boys.

FOD, for us, was something we had to take into consideration on a daily basis, and at other times, like when we were thinking of traveling, for example, but we decided long ago we were not going to let this diagnosis define us! Our boys' FOD is a long-chain transporter defect. Because it is long-chain, it takes longer for their bodies to have an issue. There are many different FODs, and for some families, this is much more difficult to deal with, having to feed around the clock or deal with complications that were caused from the initial illness before the diagnosis. Kids can have muscle tone issues and energy issues. If the FOD is a short-chain, or medium-chain type, the disorder is much more complicated. Many children die from undiagnosed or misdiagnosed FODs every year. Newborn screenings are a tool that helps to identify many of these hidden disorders. Like Dr. L. said to us when Joe had been ill, it was a miracle he was still here and unharmed. I believe it was because of this that we felt so blessed and that, since we had made it through that ordeal, we could handle whatever the world could throw at us. We were not going to let this diagnosis restrict what we liked to do, to the degree that we could, and to the degree that we could keep them safe. It was not going to become our lives. It was part of us, but it would not define us! It would not limit the boys or us! Well, OK, they could never go on a TV show like *Survivor*, but other than that … In making this decision, I decided that this also meant having the family we had dreamed of. I loved my boys more than anything in this whole world, and that was why I still wanted to have another child. I also thought it might be fun to have a girl because I had not experienced that yet. I was also open to having another boy. I honestly can say I just felt our family picture was not yet complete. We had said we wanted three or four children. When we finally were pregnant the second time, Paul had said, "OK, can we change our minds? We can just have two, the same gender, that way they can wear hand-me-downs, and then we can be done." *Ha ha, funny guy!*

Honestly, if I had felt that I was done, I would have agreed. But the truth was, when I looked at the beautiful picture of our two boys, I always felt there was something, or rather someone, missing. I had an inner desire, an inner drive to have another baby. I would not be living from love but from fear if I let this disorder dictate my dreams. I grew up with one brother, and my husband had one sister and one brother. I had always dreamed of what it would have been like if I'd had a sister. I love my brother; he is the best and always looked after me and out for me. We still have fun together to this day. I just always wondered. And now it was my turn to have my own family. If the only reason to not have more kids was because of the metabolic disorder, then I would be living from fear! How was I supposed to set an example of living from love if I did that?

Shania Twain's song, "You're Still the One," became our family's song. Between Joe's survival and the arrival of Colby, we felt we had beaten the odds together, and we were so in love with each other, with our boys, and with our family. This song reminded me to always look at what we would be missing if we hadn't had faith, trusted, and believed in our hearts, and if I hadn't listened to my inner voice and followed my inner desires. I was so glad that I had listened to intuition instead of the voices from outside of us.

I was so glad we didn't listen to the fear but listened to the love within our hearts. I could not imagine not being in this life or not having any of these beautiful people in my life. Even with this understanding, there were times during these challenges when we had doubted if we were supposed to be together. We had wondered if all this had been a sign that we were not supposed to be married or have kids. Or maybe, just maybe, it was a sign that we were supposed to be together! How could this beautiful, loving family be wrong? It could not, and I now knew we could get through anything together, or so I thought.

The next few years would challenge this belief. It would push us to the brink and test our resolve once more. Would we be able to make it? Would we each still be the one the other wanted for life?

## CHAPTER 6

# The Hope Stone

• • • • • • • • • •

Once my babies were close to two years old, I would start getting baby fever again. Knowing that I had challenges, and wanting my next child to be closer in age than the almost five years separating my boys now, we started a little earlier. I started charting my cycles again in May, when Colby was now about one and a half years old.

Because of my past early miscarriages, my doctor had suggested I use progesterone again to help me achieve and keep a pregnancy. Progesterone supplements can also make your cycle longer because you do not start your period naturally. You also must take pregnancy tests to know if you should stop taking the progesterone and allow your body to start its natural menstruation, or if you are pregnant, to continue in the hopes of helping your body maintain the proper level of progesterone to support the pregnancy.

The fertility cycle charts take note of your waking, or basal, temperature. This is a huge indicator of ovulation. You also need to make note of different indicators from your body, and how long your luteal phase is. The luteal phase is the length from ovulation to menses, the average being twelve to fourteen days. When you ovulate, the naturally occurring hormone progesterone causes your temperature to rise, and it will stay high for the remainder of the luteal phase, dropping just before your period starts. If you are pregnant, it will stay high. This is why you track your temperature to determine the best time to conceive, and to tell if conception has occurred. Every woman should know these things about her own body, and I could not believe I had not known these signs and indicators my whole life!

My normal cycle lasted, on average, twenty-eight to thirty days, and I was regular, meaning it did not vary from this by more than a day or so. However, the longest progesterone-induced cycle I experienced was thirty-six days with no pregnancy. It was the first cycle I charted again. I took multiple negative urine tests at home and then confirmed with a negative blood pregnancy test from the doctor's office before stopping the progesterone. For the next nine months, I charted my temperature; my bodily signs; how I slept; the best time for and when we tried to conceive; how long my luteal phases were; when I took progesterone; when my periods started and ended; and if I'd had a cold, a beer, or anything and everything that could affect my monthly cycle and my fertility.

It was January, now nine months since trying to conceive again, on the fifteenth day of my luteal phase. Having had some nausea and upset stomach issues the day before and no dip in my temperature to indicate an impending start to my menstruation, I took an early pregnancy urine test at home at 7:00 p.m. It was positive. Two days later, with temperatures remaining high, I took another test and got another positive result. The second line was light, but it was there. Six days later, my breasts felt full, and I was tired. These are all positive signs of pregnancy for me.

Now, when you take progesterone, you need to wear pads because you insert it like a tampon, and it does not all get absorbed into your body, and it comes out. It is very messy. I noticed on the next day some light red spotting on my panty liner and progesterone applicator. There was a brownish color to my liner in the morning. The next day, day twenty-five of my luteal phase and day forty of my cycle, the spotting stopped! I was indeed pregnant! On February 9, two days later on the progesterone suppositories, I started bleeding and cramping. I had miscarried at just six week's gestation. My temperature did not drop naturally because I was taking the progesterone suppositories, but once I had miscarried, I stopped taking it, and my temperatures began to fall.

I had a longer-than-normal period of about eight days. And, surprised by my own charting, we tried to conceive again right away. I started right back up with the progesterone on the nineteenth day of my cycle, with a negative pregnancy test on day twenty-eight, and I stopped the

49

progesterone. Still no period on day thirty, so I took another pregnancy test, but it was still negative. It was a thirty-one-day cycle. I was obviously a woman on a mission. I was not going to let this get the better of me. For the next two months I charted, but we went on vacation in April, so I took time off from all the charting but started back up again in May. I would start the progesterone suppositories after ovulation and take a pregnancy test around day twenty-eight or thirty of my cycle to know if I was pregnant and needed to keep taking the progesterone or not. I had done this for four months since the last miscarriage in February but had not gotten pregnant again.

Six months after my last miscarriage, I stopped charting. It was June, and I started to seek alternative methods to improve my fertility. I started reading a lot. *The Infertility Cure*, by Randine Lewis, PhD, became my bible. It is about ancient Chinese wellness, including herbal medicine, eating the right foods for your particular body type, and which exercises are best. I took a quiz, and the answers indicated where in my body I might be experiencing an imbalance. The book then gave diet and lifestyle suggestions, as well as acupuncture, herbs, and exercise to improve my fertility. It told me what types of foods I should eat to improve not only fertility but overall health and well-being.

I started exercising regularly. Fertility yoga was my choice. It was extremely calming and made my body feel great! I also stopped drinking alcohol, as I read this can also interfere with fertility, and I started going to an acupuncturist. Acupuncture can help stimulate the flow of blood to areas of the body. For the purpose of helping with fertility, it can boost blood flow to reproductive organs and can balance hormones. This book gave me back control of my body. It gave me practical steps, as well as actionable physical and mental things, like meditation, to help myself. It also gave me information about massaging meridian points on my own, as well as points that an acupuncturist could use. This helped me because I was not just going to an acupuncturist and blindly following what he or she told me. I was understanding it myself.

This book gave me back my power. It also gave information to help support Western fertility treatments. It gave me the bigger picture, of not just ancient Chinese wellness or Western invasive treatments, but a way that I and any reader could use the ancient methods to support the fertility treatments so they could work together. It is the most comprehensive and open-minded practical guide to taking charge of your own fertility that I have ever come across. Randine Lewis encourages her readers to follow what makes sense to them, and this perhaps was the best advice I have ever gotten.

Randine wrote, "Ultimately no matter what path or paths we choose in our pursuit of fertility we must be willing to take command of our own medical care. We must not rely on the word of any one medical tradition or practitioner. Above all we must learn to listen to our own body, mind, soul, and heart." In *Inconceivable*, by Julia Indichova, Christiane Northrup, MD, the author of *Women's Bodies, Women's Wisdom*, writes: "When we're willing to listen to our bodies and begin trusting ourselves as much as we trust outer authorities, all the rules change. And so does our biology. Statistics no longer apply to us. We enter the realm of miracles and undreamed-of possibilities."

I also recommend reading *Inconceivable*, by Julia Indichova. In her book, she also emphasizes following what works for each individual and to follow our own truth. Because of the journey I have already been on with the near death of my eldest child, this spoke to my soul, and I knew how to trust my own wisdom from within. I knew how to tune in and follow what resonated with me, what I knew I could handle, and what I knew I could not. I also learned to try things. If I was not sure, I soon would figure out what my mind and body were capable of. These two books, along with others that spoke to me (some more than others), gave me back my control, gave me my own inner guide to follow, and I learned more about what I was capable of and what I was willing to do to conceive another child.

According to the questions from *The Infertility Cure*, it indicated that I needed to consume warm foods, and I was to avoid cold foods, excess dairy, and sugar. I also ate mostly all-organic foods, and hormone-free meats. The book said I should exercise moderately and meditate to help relieve worry and stress. I watched a lot of comedy shows and movies. Also, I dove into many other books about boosting fertility and preventing miscarriages. I was trying to understand why my body was doing what it was doing, in an attempt to bring it back into balance and achieve and maintain a healthy pregnancy. After all, I had two beautiful boys; certainly, I could conceive and carry another baby to term. Or could I? When something is not going how you would like or how you had planned, you sometimes cannot help but let doubt slip in. Doubt would creep in at times, because otherwise my desired outcome would have worked by now, right?

I spent the summer getting my mind, body, and soul in balance. I was enjoying my boys. Joe was going to a baseball camp. We had dropped him off for a half-day camp in the morning, and Colby and I were walking hand in hand back through the gravel drive toward our car. The issues I was having were often, if not constantly, on my mind. Your life ends up revolving around your monthly cycle, literally! I did a lot of soul-searching and reading, as I have already told you. These other women's stories were very compelling. I sometimes had days of doubt, or even sadness, but I would always be happy with my children. I loved them so very much, and it was actually because of them that I so desired to have another child. There were times when even family members would say things like, "Can't you just be happy with what you have?" They did not understand that had nothing to do with it. I was not desiring to have another child because I was not happy with the children I already had, or my life, or any of that. It was quite the contrary, and it was because I was so happy with my children and my husband, and our life, that I so desired to bring another into it.

Because even well-meaning family say these insensitive things, not realizing the stupidity of what they are actually saying, it can plant tiny seeds of doubt. Was I being selfish? Would my children think I wasn't happy with them? Was I doing the right thing? And then, because it was not happening naturally, it also planted doubt. *If it was meant to be, why hasn't it happened yet? Is there something wrong with me? Should I just give up?* Of course, I could be happy with my boys; they are the best! Why was this so important to me? As Colby and I walked to the car, all these thoughts were swimming around in my head at the same time. I was questioning myself, my motives, and my inner desires.

As I was thinking these thoughts, I looked down and saw a rock about two inches across with the word HOPE stamped in it. In this sea of gravel and rocks all about, encompassing a wide drive with space for multiple cars, I looked down at the exact moment that allowed me to see the word HOPE next to my foot. I did not step on it, but next to it. I got goose bumps and butterflies in my stomach, and I felt giddy all at the same time. I bent down to pick it up and rubbed it in my hand. I felt the smoothness of the rock with the rough edges of the letters on one side. I looked up and around and said, "Thank you!"

I knew this was a wink from the universe. I could not have found that HOPE rock if I had been trying. I would never have been able to see it among all the others, but for some reason, I had looked down at the exact moment that allowed me to do just that. The universe had heard my questions and sent me an answer. And it renewed my faith in Spirit, and in my own inner wisdom. It gave me hope that I was supposed to have another child, and that it would all be OK. I kept that rock for years. Many people call them worry rocks, but I call them wishing rocks. I would rather wish and be hopeful than worry any day!

I started charting again in October. I also started testing the luteinizing hormone (LH) with an at-home test. A surge in this hormone is what triggers ovulation about a day or a day and a half later. This is a good indicator to time conception. It is an ovulation predictor kit, and it works the same as a pregnancy test, but it indicates impending ovulation, and therefore, the best times for conception. This test, along with all the information from using the guidelines in *The Infertility Cure*, gave me the utmost confidence to understand my body and to corroborate the evidence I was seeing with the science of testing my hormone levels. All indicators said I was ovulating. A progesterone deficiency can be indicated by early miscarriage, which is also why I continued to take progesterone supplements. However, unfortunately, it was not working, and my OB suggested it was time to go back to the fertility doctors.

It had been a year and a half since I had started trying to conceive again, and eleven months of no pregnancies, despite everything I was doing. November was my first month back with the fertility doctors, the same ones I thought did not know what the (bleep) they were doing. They started me back on the Clomid and they tested all my hormone levels. They tested my follicle-stimulating hormone (FSH) and estradiol levels to indicate if ovulation was occurring. They also performed a hysterosalpingography (HSG). This is a test that uses X-rays and a dye injected into the uterus and fallopian tubes to make sure there is nothing blocking the tubes or preventing a fertilized egg from implanting properly. They also take blood levels to help indicate what is going on. The HSG is performed after your period but before ovulation. In my case, they did it on my day eight or nine, and it showed no blockages, but the day-ten blood work showed that I had already ovulated. Just to make sure nothing had changed, they also scheduled a semen analysis for my husband later in the month.

Another issue was that I had started getting my period when I was eleven years old. Although I was twenty-seven when I'd had Joe, thirty-two when I'd had Colby, and was now only thirty-five, my biological age, especially that of my fertility, could be older since I'd started my cycles so young. All the tests indicated no known issues. So why wasn't I getting pregnant? I was doing all the right things and felt a renewed sense that following my inner desire was the right path for me. I was not going to give up. However, I was also concerned that conceiving on our own was going to end in miscarriage. I did not want to think this; it was just there in the back of my mind because of my history. I came to grips with going back to get help from the fertility doctors. I now had an understanding of how the Eastern methods could support the Western methods when it came to fertility. I was more open-minded about the whole process this time, and I thought that maybe using the Eastern and Western approaches together would be the best way to have a healthy child in the long run. Why would I miscarry so early? I did not know if it went beyond a progesterone deficiency. Maybe using the Western fertility methods would weed out the eggs that would not produce a healthy baby. Maybe this, along with all the organic food, acupuncture, yoga, and mental destressing, would be the best combination to finally achieve a healthy pregnancy and baby. I did not know for sure; all I knew was that what I had been doing was not working on its own. I did not know what else to do, and at least this time I had HOPE!

---

CHAPTER 7

# The Suckhole of Infertility

. . . . . . . . . .

It was January again, and I started my first cycle of intrauterine inseminations, or IUI. This is a process in which they insert the sperm directly into the uterus with a thin, tubelike catheter. I was still taking my health into my own hands by following the ancient Chinese wellness program from Randine Lewis's book, doing fertility yoga, and getting acupuncture treatments. I was feeling good and very hopeful! I thought this could be the answer.

In my case, the IUI also included fertility drugs to increase the number of eggs I would produce. My husband would have to make a sample in a sterile cup and then bring it to the office in the morning. They then "cleaned" my husband's sperm. This process is done to help eliminate the slower moving or dead sperm and allow for the healthier sperm to have a better chance of survival and fertilization. In this cycle, they inseminated me with my husband's "washed" sperm on two consecutive days. They then would give me a pregnancy test after two weeks if I had not gotten my period yet. No need to test me this month, as I got my period eleven days later.

The next cycle was one that challenged us and pushed us beyond what we thought we would ever do. I started with the fertility meds on day three of my next cycle. I needed to keep taking the shots daily until the eggs were the proper size. Then Paul would give me the human chorionic gonadotropin or HCG shot to release the eggs and cause ovulation. This was the big one in the butt. The other shots were smaller, and I could put them in my thigh on my own. However, I never thought I would also be self-inseminating.

We realized when we were getting everything ready for the morning that Paul had not been given a sterile cup to use. It was much too late to get one from the office; they were closed. He called the doctor on call, who assured us we could just sterilize a plastic container with a cover, and it would be fine. So, first thing in the morning, Paul sterilized a container, and then "did his thing," and brought it to the doctor's office. He called me on his way back to say that they said we could not use the sample because it was not in a sterile cup from the office. He had explained how we had spoken with the doctor on call, and he had told us what to do. However, the nurses said that the specimen was suboptimal, and they gave us instructions to have IC (intercourse). They said to return to the clinic in three days for IUI. I told him to bring that stuff home; we were not going to waste it, or this entire cycle. I had taken the shots for the last five days. We had already done the HCG shot we knew would cause me to ovulate, and there was at least one egg measuring eighteen by eighteen millimeters. The rest had been thirteen to fourteen millimeters. So I said, "F— it! Where's the turkey baster?"

I'm not kidding, that stuff is like gold. The sperm was not washed, but the motility of the sperm was never the issue. I was not going through all those shots for nothing. I went in my room, propped myself up on a pillow with my uterus tilted, and I inseminated myself. I had sterilized the turkey baster, and we knew the container was sterile, even though the doctors did not want to trust it! I lay there for about thirty minutes after, just to make sure the "guys" and "gals" had time to swim without gravity pulling them in the other direction. We then also had sex that night, and again the next morning and night, to optimize the chances of pregnancy, and because we were unable to return to the clinic for the rest of the IUI because of a snowstorm.

It was a good thing they had instructed us to have IC! Because we did not know to do this? (Insert sarcasm here.) Honestly, we went to them for help with fertility, and they forgot to give us a sterile cup, and then they gave us instructions to have IC. Thanks for nothing! We only told two people about the turkey baster; one being my mom, because she had been there to watch the boys for us before we were told to take our suboptimal sperm home. The other was my friend Betsey, who had called during all the chaos, and of course, I had to let her in on the shenanigans. She said if we became pregnant from this cycle, she would give our kid the nickname Giblets. She may have even suggested that as the legal name, but she also asked to please never invite her to Thanksgiving dinner.

The jokes and looks that flew around between my mom, Paul, and me the next Thanksgiving when basting the turkey were hard to hide. Oh, and sorry to our family with whom we ate turkey that year, who are just finding this out now. Relax, we did get a new turkey baster, if you were wondering. It was funny, and something we look back on and laugh about. Also, I do not suggest doing this. I am only sharing this crazy information to show just how desperate I became when I could not control my world, and to let other women know that, when you feel like this, you are not alone. But please do not try this at home; it was actually a very risky thing to do because of possible infection. However, I do suggest always having a good sense of humor about it all, as this will take you far. Unfortunately, it did not take this time either. There was no child named Giblets in our future. We would go through a total of three IUI cycles with no luck.

IUI is used as the first treatment for unexplained infertility, along with the ovulating-inducing medicine with the hope of resulting in a "normal" pregnancy. We had done everything. We had come so far, with nothing to show for it. I could not believe that I would have such a strong desire to have another child if it were not possible. I could not understand why this was happening. I honestly thought this would work.

Before we started with all the shots, I thought I couldn't do it. I did not think I could handle it. When we were told that this was the next step at a meeting at the office, I had to excuse myself to the bathroom, where I promptly began to cry silently in a type of anxiety attack. I had to pull myself together quickly and do slow, deep breathing before I could return to the instructional group meeting. Every time I took another step into the possible answer to my problem, I also felt I was getting a little farther away from my truth. I was believing one thing and being told another.

I had spent all this time getting myself healthy, only to put artificial drugs into my body now. This is the way you get pregnant when it is not working. Right? They told me this was what I should do, and they are the professionals, so I took the Clomid, and we induced multiple egg production, and we induced ovulation, and we "washed" the sperm, and we sterilized everything, even our relationship! I charted, and we scheduled, and we made it work. We scheduled sex: when to do it and when not to do it, because I could not be pregnant when starting some procedures, or the unthinkable could happen. I made my body cycle predictable, and we tried IUI cycles with breaks in between cycles so I didn't stress my body. But none of it had worked, so they said the next thing to do was in vitro fertilization (IVF). We still had one more IUI cycle approved by insurance, and we had to follow the insurance protocol before they would approve IVF cycles. Since it had not worked up to that point, the doctors were not overly optimistic about this last IUI cycle.

I had taken a long break, about seven months. I was also working as a preschool teacher, and I was raising my two boys. Some days, I don't know how I managed to fit it all in. It is crazy to look back and think about how regular it all became, just another part of my daily life. One morning, I was at work waiting to get the call back from the nurse to say if it was time for the HCG shot. I was on my break, using the ladies' room, and wearing my husband's big Red Sox sweatshirt for "red day," or "sports day," or whatever day it was, I forget. I had my phone in the front pocket of the zip-up hoodie. And as I stood up with the oversized sweatshirt bunched up around my waist, pulling up my pants, I heard a splash. I had a panic attack and looked down into the toilet. There, along with my urine, was my phone! I did not even hesitate.

I flew my hand into that toilet and retrieved that damn phone, while simultaneously having a heart attack! I started freaking out. *How am I going to get the call? What if they call me while I'm still here, and my phone doesn't work?* You are at their beck and call because they call and leave a message, and they are only at the fertility clinic for set hours in the morning, and then you can't get a hold of them. As all of this was going through my head, I had a class of about eight four-year-olds, and my aide was waiting for me to return to class. *Of all days to drop my phone into the toilet! The day I may have to induce ovulation ... WTF! I cannot believe I just did that.*

Finally, in December, we tried our last IUI cycle with no luck. In February they scheduled a hysteroscopy to rule out endometrial polyps. Endometrial polyps are small, soft growths on the inside of a woman's uterus. They can be associated with decreased pregnancy rates as well as miscarriages. Polyps can also interfere with sperm transport and embryo implantation. I have had issues with all of these, and since I was still diagnosed with unexplained infertility, and the next step was IVF, endometrial polyps had to be ruled out before proceeding. Fortunately, everything looked normal, and we were given the go-ahead for the next step, IVF.

This time, they would remove my eggs and use my husband's sperm to create an embryo in the lab at the hospital, and then they would put the embryo or embryos back in my body. This was the next step. What else could I do? Although I hated the idea of putting all these drugs into my body, I was confident that I had done my best to be at my healthiest, and I hoped that this, along with the IVF procedure, would allow me to finally have the positive outcome I was looking for.

I started the shots on the days they told me and at the dosages they gave me. Then I would have ultrasounds and blood levels taken to determine the size of the eggs and when to take the HCG shot that tells my body to release the eggs. Next, I had to go into the hospital and have a procedure under anesthesia to retrieve the developing eggs. And, of course, they needed the sperm from my husband, so he would have to supply that. After the egg retrieval, they would be fertilized with the sperm and allowed to grow for three days. This was the craziest thing! The doctors were making our baby in a hospital, outside of our bodies, with parts from our bodies for the next three days, while we were somewhere else doing other things. Science is amazing! Our parts were somewhere else, mixing together and creating our baby. It was exciting and nerve-racking all at the same time.

During the first IVF cycle, they retrieved four eggs for fertilization. We got the phone call that only one had taken and created an embryo. I was like, "Let's *go!*" When I called my mom to tell her, I said, "All we need is one!" Obviously, we had been told about the risks of multiples with this procedure. So, although the idea of twins was exciting, it was also comforting to only have one fertilized egg being implanted. I knew it could still split into twins, but that was an even rarer occurrence. We were so excited. I thought this was it! This was how our baby would finally come to us.

I had to wait about ten days for them to take the blood for my pregnancy test. It was positive! We were pregnant. The nurse warned me that my numbers were a little low, however, and this could be a sign that the pregnancy might not be viable, meaning that it would end in miscarriage. I was like, "Oh, hell no!" I said to her, "Well, I'm going to stay positive! I feel really good, and I'm going to be optimistic!"

The next day, she called me with my numbers, and she said, "You were right, they are bouncing back!" The numbers are hormone levels indicating pregnancy, the HCG, and they should double every two days or so. If they are slow to go up, then the pregnancy might not be progressing properly, and if they are going down, you are having a miscarriage.

I was scheduled for my ultrasound the following week. Over the weekend I had excruciating pain in my left side, but it was not constant. I had been told that if it was a constant pain, it might be worrisome, but this came and went. It was very painful at times. I was pacing around my bedroom, and all I could think was, *I can't lose this baby!* I just could not handle even the thought of it. The next day, the pain was gone. I was so relieved when it subsided, and I figured it had been gas. Gas in your intestine can cause severe lower abdomen pain. My numbers were still multiplying the way they should, and I felt great now that the side pain had subsided.

Paul went to work, and I got the boys off to school and went to my ultrasound appointment. I went in, and I was laying with the waist of my pants below my hips. The ultrasound technician came in and put the jelly-like lubricant on my tummy and started moving the transducer around on my abdomen. I was all excited and was waiting for her to show me the first glimpse of our little one. However, she was taking a rather long time. As I watched, her facial expression was one of concern, not joy. I felt like I had just gotten punched in the gut. This wave of horrified emotion came over me. I did not dare ask what was wrong. I was too frightened.

Finally, she cut through the tension in the air by saying, "Do you have an appointment with the doctor today?"

I answered, "No, I don't. I'm not scheduled to see the doctor today. Why?"

She replied, "I'll be back in a minute." And she left the room.

Now I was having a full-blown panic attack again, as I was laying in an ultrasound room in the dark, by myself. *WTF? WTF is wrong now?* They had me dress and go into a room with the nurse. The nurse then went on to explain that the technician could not see a developing embryo or sac in my uterus. There was nothing there, but my numbers were saying I was pregnant. It was not another blighted ovum because the sac would have been there, just with nothing developing in it.

I started sobbing and trying to explain that, as soon as the tech had asked me if I had an appointment that day, I knew something was very wrong. They then asked if anyone was with me that day to drive me home. I said, "Um, no." This was supposed to be the happiest day of my life, and I was gonna drive home and show Paul the sonogram pictures of our baby. They wanted me to get another ultrasound done at the hospital, to see if they could figure out what was going on. They suspected a tubal pregnancy, which is a slightly higher risk than normal with IVF procedures, because the embryo can float around for a longer period of time before implantation. An ectopic pregnancy is a pregnancy that implants outside of the uterus. A tubal pregnancy is an ectopic pregnancy that implants in the fallopian tube. At this time, I was still not putting together the pain I'd had previously, as I still thought that had been just gas, and that an ectopic pregnancy would have continued to be painful and possibly cause bleeding.

I do not remember how I got home. All I know is that Paul and I went together to the ultrasound office at the hospital. It was full of happy couples and families waiting for their names to be called, to see their developing fetus on the big screen. I was so distraught and overcome by immense sadness. I just sat, not able to hold back the tears as they streamed down my cheeks, with my head on Paul's chest as we waited for our names to be called, knowing we were not going to get to see our fetus. I kept thinking, *We should be in a different room. We should be in the sad room. We should not have to see these people's happy faces and hear their laughter of joy.* It was unbearable.

Once again, I was on the table, with the hospital technician now using the transducer and jelly on my abdomen. She did not see anything, but she mentioned my gallbladder was very oddly shaped. I was like, "OK, whatever, does that really matter right now?"

She then called the doctor over to use the transducer and see if he could find my pregnancy. He had no luck but corroborated the fact that my gallbladder was oddly shaped. If I had not thought I was in the twilight zone earlier, I definitely thought I was there now. *What is going on? People, we are looking for a lost pregnancy, not oddly shaped organs! Can you stick to the task at hand, please? For the love of Pete!*

They sent me to the emergency room, where a very nice, young male nurse explained what was happening. Apparently, they could not find the pregnancy. However, they knew that I'd had an IVF procedure, and according to my blood levels, my body was acting like it was pregnant. Since the pregnancy was not in the uterus, it would not be a viable pregnancy. He needed to give me a shot in my ass. It was a methotrexate shot, to rid my body of any remaining "products of conception." The drug inhibits growth of the fertilized egg. This can help reduce the chances of it continuing to grow if it is in the tube, which could cause the tube to burst, and cause a life-threatening situation for the mom (in this case, me). He sent us home with specific instructions to return to the ER if I was bleeding too much. Too much bleeding meant going through a pad or more in an hour. If this happened, it could mean I was hemorrhaging, another potentially life-threatening situation. We understood his instructions, and we returned home with plans to repeat my HCG levels on Friday and then again on Monday. The official diagnosis was a probable ectopic or spontaneous abortion, which is the technical term for a miscarriage. The doctor's notes mentioned ectopic precautions. We were so incredibly sad and dejected by the whole ordeal.

## CHAPTER 8

# The Tubal and the Tumor

· · · · · · · · ·

It was extremely late by the time we got home, and we went straight to bed. It wasn't until later the next day that I realized I was bleeding way too much. We waited a little while. I did not want to overreact, but it was not subsiding. We decided we had no choice; we must go back, to be on the safe side. Now I was sad and scared.

We headed back into the ER where we were made to wait for what seemed like an excruciatingly long period of time. It was now two days since my methotrexate shot, and I was in some serious pain on my left side. The doctor was lacking in bedside manners, and he came in and asked me why I was crying. Paul was like, "Jesus, man, do you not get what is going on here?"

The doctor said, "I'm just trying to assess if you are crying out of emotional pain or physical pain."

Paul and I said at the same time, *"Both!"* And yes, I was in extreme pain on my left side. Thankfully, the technicians were on top of their game. I was now in the ER, behind a curtain in an area where they had the ultrasound machine. Paul was holding my hand, and tears were constantly leaking from my eyes. The transducer was being pushed around on my abdomen, and when they got to the left side, it hurt like hell.

There were three technicians, each trying to help figure out what was going on. They were talking back and forth with each other, one on the transducer and one on the monitor and one watching everything very closely. Suddenly, one of them yelled out, "There! There it is! There's the heartbeat!"

Paul and I gasped! I shuddered with sobs of pain and grief. They had finally found our lost baby. They even showed Paul the tiny heartbeat as tears were streaming down his face.

I think sometimes people in the medical field forget they are working with people's lives. It was as if they had found a missing piece to a puzzle. I guess that is, in a sense, what they had done. They had solved the mystery. What I could not believe was that, somehow, this little "product of conception," our baby, was still growing after the methotrexate shot. He or she was somehow still there, but the reality was that we would never get to meet this baby. We would never get to hold the tiny hands and kiss the little toes and smell the sweet breath of this newborn, because although he or she existed for us in every way imaginable, he or she would never get the opportunity to live. This glimpse of the heartbeat that Paul got to see would be the only memory we would have of this one's life.

Oh, and to make matters worse, if you can imagine, one technician said, "You know, you don't have an oddly shaped gallbladder; you have a very large cyst on your gallbladder, and you're going to have to have that looked at, immediately."

*Excuse me. Um, what? Are you f—ing kidding me?*

I was then wheeled back into my curtained-off room where we both continued to wipe our tears and face our fears and wait for my operation to remove the ectopic pregnancy and fallopian tube. We would have to wait to find out what the grapefruit-size cyst was that had enveloped my gallbladder.

As they prepped me for surgery, we asked if they could just take the cyst out while they were in there. Get it all over and done with in one shot. We were joking, but not. They unfortunately said no, we had to have it diagnosed before anything could be done. I just wanted my baby back, I wanted my life back, I wanted me back. I did not know what the future held for me, except that I was not going to have another baby now. Maybe not ever. This was now an emergency surgery situation. From the ultrasound, they knew the heartbeat meant the methotrexate shot had not worked, and the tube could still burst. Before they took me into surgery, they asked us if we wanted "it."

We looked at each other, and agreed no, not to take it. It was so sad. I wanted to scream, "Yes, of course, I want my baby!" I wanted my pregnancy, I wanted my baby, but what would I do? I am sure some people have a religious ceremony, but that just was not us. How do I bring it home and explain this to my children? No, I could not bring my sadness, my knowledge of these horrible things that can happen, home to my children. *No, I do not want them to know their brother or sister had died before he or she ever even got a chance to live. No, I will protect my kids from that sadness.* It had been hard enough when I had told Joe I was having a baby, then had a miscarriage, and my nephew told the stranger at the park that I had lost my baby. I could not, and would not, put this sadness and knowledge on them. They needed to stay blissfully ignorant as to how cruel life can be at times. They needed to have their mom home safe and sound with them.

My priority now had to be taking care of myself, for my own sake, but also for my husband and my two boys. I needed to be healthy, and right now, we had no idea what this growth around my gallbladder was. I had thought I was so healthy. I had no way of knowing this thing was growing inside of me. While I would occasionally have pain in that area, just to the inside of my ribs, I had also been in a car accident years ago, and my ribs had struck the steering wheel. I just always figured it was some scar tissue from that, because I never remembered it hurting before the accident. I had now had two full-term pregnancies, one born at seven pounds nine ounces, and the other at nine pounds twelve ounces. I did not think that it could have been there then. There would have been no room. There were so many unknowns for the moment. It was time for surgery.

Everything went as expected. They did end up taking the tube, which they had discussed with us prior. According to the doctor's notes, there had been blood at the end of the tube, but there was still a mass in the tube, so it was best to remove it all. According to the radiology report, they removed my left tube and the "products of conception" (POC). There was a gestational sac measuring 1.5 centimeters by 1.5 centimeters and containing a yolk sac, and a 3-millimeter embryo with a fetal heart rate (FHR) of 93 beats per minute. The impression notes stated I had a left adnexal ectopic pregnancy with a live embryo. "With live embryo." I can't even! It had worked. We had conceived a baby through IVF, but it could not live. What kind of cruel irony was this?

Overwhelming grief consumed me. And now I had to face my own mortality. I needed to know what this growth was. Could it be cancer? Would I be OK? I had to come to the realization that there was nothing I could do about losing this baby. No amount of tears in the world would bring him or her back. My health had to become my focus now.

My primary care doctor sent me to a gastroenterologist who did lab tests and a CT scan to try and figure out what we were dealing with. He was able to determine that I had a large, basically fluid-filled mass, but with many chambers and debris. The bile ducts and the pancreatic ducts seemed normal, but the gallbladder itself was not visible. He quickly realized I needed someone more specialized, and he referred me to a doctor at Boston Medical Center. He was a biliary disorder specialist, a doctor who focuses on the biliary system, which includes bile ducts, the gallbladder, and structures that are involved with the production and transportation of bile. It was possible that this was a biliary cystadenoma, which is a rare, benign tumor primarily diagnosed in middle-aged women. However, I only had abdominal pain off and on, and I had none of the other symptoms. The mass was not palpable, and I was not jaundiced, all symptoms of the tumor.

On the day of my appointment I met the assistant, not the doctor. They had not told me to bring any pictures, so I had not. Once there, he asked me for them. No one had told me to bring them, and this would have been an important detail to mention to me. He then proceeded very abruptly in his manner, and I honestly do not remember ever actually meeting the doctor. He had been held up in a surgery or something. I was not feeling it, and at this point, as you know, I have learned to listen to my gut instincts. I called my primary care doctor in tears, begging her to give me someone else I could go to. I had known my primary care doctor since I was eleven, when my cycles had started, and she was wonderful. So she obliged and sent me to someone else.

This doctor was at the Beth Israel Deaconess Medical Center in Boston. He was actually a transplant doctor. I was like, *Great, overqualified works for me!* And, at the same time, I was hoping that did not mean I would be needing any kind of transplant. The scheduling secretaries, the nurses, the assistants, and even the custodians were genuinely kind and caring people. I was so much more comfortable with this doctor; he was an extremely knowledgeable and kind man. I had to have a number of tests done: MRI, CT scan, and an endoscopic retrograde cholangiopancreatography (ERCP). An ERCP is an exam that uses an endoscope and X-ray to put a little camera down through your throat and into your stomach and ducts to assess the situation. The camera gives important information, more than the ultrasound, MRI, and CT scans can provide. It would be a big help in diagnosing what this was.

On the morning of my ERCP, my mom drove me in and stayed with me. We left early, but we hit no traffic, so we were an hour early. The city has a peaceful quiet about it, early in the morning before it awakens with the hustle and bustle of life. It was summer and warm out, and it was quiet among the shadows of the tall buildings, and we sat and talked and laughed. My mom could always make me laugh, especially when I was stressed out. She had a way of just making something funny. I don't even remember the exact conversation, but I will never forget how she made me feel! Relaxed, at ease, loved, and much calmer. When it was my turn, the hospital had awoken and was now a rumble of nurses and doctors doing their jobs, and patients waiting their turns. They had these procedures down to a T. I had my IV and was getting ready to go in. The next thing I knew, I was awake in the recovery area. I woke up and said, "How did it go?"

My mom said, "It didn't."

One of the nurses started calling me Rocky. I looked at my mom, still confused. They proceeded to tell me that, while I was under anesthesia, when they had tried to put the tube down my throat, I'd started swinging at the doctors and nurses. I was punching at them and would not let them do the procedure. I was so embarrassed, but I was now also laughing. My mom was cracking up. The guy next to me was a big guy, like over six feet tall, and two hundred pounds. He was in great shape, and the nurse asked me why I couldn't be cooperative like he was, with a smile on her face, just giving me a hard time. He was quiet and calm as a lamb. But I—at five foot four inches and 123 pounds—was a force to be reckoned with. I could not believe I had done that, and I was so apologetic. I tried my hardest to convince them that I was really a nice person!

They eventually did a CAT scan on me. It showed the cross-sectional images, or slices, of the cyst, like a loaf of bread. It was quite fascinating to see, and quite mind-blowing to think this huge thing was inside of me. The good news was it was not cancerous. It was benign, whatever *it* was. Paul and I had one brief conversation concerning the possibility of cancer, and we had decided not to go there and to instead keep a positive outlook, no matter what. Somewhere in the recesses of my mind, I knew that, even if it were malignant, I would overcome it. The scariest part is the not knowing. Well, now we knew that it was not cancerous, so what the heck was it? Since they were not able to get any information from the ERCP, we needed to proceed with caution.

The doctor decided that the best line of action was to not do laparoscopic surgery. Laparoscopic is when they make small incisions in the abdomen and go in with a fiber-optic instrument to do the surgical procedure. This type of surgery leaves minimal scarring, but because they were unsure if the cyst could be extracted by this method, he opted for the old-fashioned method. He would perform an open gallbladder surgery. I would have a large scar across my abdomen. This was the least of my concerns, honestly. I was totally fine with it.

The day of the surgery came, and my mom and my husband came with me. I promised my husband I would give him a kiss before I went in. The male nurse who was taking care of me asked if I wanted an epidural. I had not gotten an epidural with the delivery of either of my two children. I did not like the idea of them. I had seen shows about them, and I knew how precise they have to be because if they miss by even a tiny bit, it could be extremely dangerous. So I told him, "No thanks, I didn't have one with either of my children."

He looked at me and explained that this would not be quick like childbirth, and that if he were having the same procedure as I was, he would get it, and he was a big guy. I appreciated his explanation and understood what he was saying, and I agreed to have it done. The next thing I knew, I was waking up in the recovery room. As soon as I saw my husband, I began to apologize because I never got to give him a kiss before I went into surgery. He said, "Yes, you did. You came and talked to me and gave me a kiss and then went in." I had no memory of this at all. Anesthesia is some crazy shit!

I had to stay in the hospital for a couple of days. The epidural moved on me, and I could feel my incision, but my right boob was completely numb. Well, hopefully it had helped somewhat before it had moved up into my chest. I did not feel horrible, so I figured it had been of some benefit. However, I had not pooped yet. They need to make sure you can go before they send you home. The nurse had given me an enema the next morning, but by the time the doctors did their rounds, I still had not gone.

The attending doctor decided to order me some milk of magnesia. For those who do not know what this is, milk of magnesia is a laxative that increases water in the intestine to induce a bowel movement. The nurse gave it to me, and I did not realize what the effects of this would be. Within a short period of time, between the enema and the milk of magnesia, I was literally running to the bathroom. Unfortunately, I did not make it completely. I was so embarrassed, I felt like an old person who could not control their bowels. When the nurse came to check on me, I explained what had happened and apologized and said they needed someone to come clean the floor. I expressed how I was scared, and I did not know if this was because of the surgery or what. She reassured me that it was because of all the medicine. She even then apologized because she knew I had gotten the enema, and then when she came back on for the next shift and realized the doctor had written for the milk of magnesia first thing in the morning, she said her first thought was, *That poor woman*. She knew what he had set me up for, and it was not a nice thing to do to me.

Then the doctor came in and asked how I was doing. I told him I was feeling alright, but still sore and tired. He then went on to say that he saw me heading to the bathroom and thought I was moving surprisingly well. I then said, "Well, if your insides were moving out of you at a hundred miles per hour, you'd move pretty good, too!" He kind of got a slight grin on his face. He knew that I knew what he had done to "help" me be ready to go home. I think they needed the bed! Fun times!

I was released to go home, and the boys got to come to the hospital to pick me up. It was good to see their little faces and feel their warm hugs. I was finally going home. At my follow-up, the doctor let us know what the thing on my gallbladder was. The technical diagnosis was a mesothelial cyst. It had been a mostly fluid-filled sac, but with some debris, and along with that, it was full of all kinds of blood vessels. If they had done a biopsy, or had tried to remove it laparoscopically, it could have bled profusely. If I had not known it was there and it kept growing, or if I were pregnant and it was still inside of me, it could have burst, and I could have had internal bleeding and could have bled to death. Although they initially said it could have been something I had from birth, we now doubted that. There was a possibility that if it had been there from birth, it had been very small to begin with and had only recently grown to the size it was now. If I had fallen and it burst, I could have bled out. If my baby had not gone ectopic, we never would have known it was there. If my pregnancy had developed normally, and it burst, since it was like an overinflated water balloon, Paul could have lost his wife and unborn baby. My boys could have lost their mom and their sibling.

The realization of the severity of this, and how it all played out, took my breath away. I had to sit back and realize all these crazy little things had lined up to save my life. Even the death of my unborn child. I realized that little spirit had been sent to save me. He or she came to me and said, "I'm not going anywhere until you see me and this tumor in my mom and you save her!" All the little synchronicities had to line up to save my life. The one embryo, how it had gone ectopic, the "weird" gallbladder, the methotrexate shot not working, the technicians who finally found the pregnancy and the cyst (and they knew what they were), the multiple ultrasounds, the number of doctors, the ERCP not happening, the bad feeling about the first surgeon, following my gut to this amazing doctor and staff. And then realizing after it was all over that I had been walking around with a ticking time bomb inside my body that had been disarmed at the last second. One of the worst things that had ever happened to me now became this amazing gift that gave me back my life, which I came so close to losing and had not even known it at the time.

I am so thankful every day to this little soul who came and sacrificed its life for mine. It was unconditional love! I close my eyes, and I can feel it in my soul! I know these things to be true, and this is my truth! *Now,* I wondered, *what do I do about this burning desire still tugging at my heartstrings?* Because this was also my truth. It was a desire from within me. I know many people would tell me to stop, but I just could not deny my inner calling to have another child. For now, it could wait, but I didn't think this feeling was going away anytime soon.

We spent a week in Nantucket that summer with the boys, enjoying the beach and riding bikes everywhere. I had to be careful when I lifted my leg over the bike in certain ways because of my incision. The days were spent playing in the warm sand and feeling the summer breezes on our faces. We ate ice cream and fried food, but I had to be careful not to overdo it in one meal. I had to watch my fat intake because the gallbladder helps you process fats, and I no longer had one. They had warned me not to have a cheeseburger, fries, and a shake because it would make me feel sick. Since I was used to eating healthy, this was not a huge challenge for me. We drank in the salty sea air, and it somehow enlivened me. When you can step outside your front door and breathe the salty sea air deep into your lungs, you just feel alive, and you know you are going to have a great day! It was a wonderful week.

One day, we went down to the beach in the cliff area. It was a cooler day, and no one else was on the beach. The boys were running, trying to catch the seagulls. All of a sudden, I heard Colby say, "Look, Mom, I caught one!" I turned around to see him patting a seagull, like you would pat a dog. He was so proud of himself. Paul and I realized at the same time what was actually going on, and we started screaming, "*No!* Stop! Get away from it!" His poor little face was so shocked. The seagull was dead, and Colby did not know it. And all we could think of was the germs! We ran back to the truck with Colby's hand outstretched until we could get some hand sanitizer on it! Ugh! Yuck! I don't think we told him it was dead, but Joe was old enough to understand. I think we told him it was sleeping. We still talk about the time Colby thought he actually caught a seagull, and he is quick to remind us he did catch one, it was just no longer alive. We always laugh about this, and it turns out it is the best medicine there is! Laughter, family, and sunshine!

---
CHAPTER 9
---

# *IVF, Facing my Fears,*
# *and Letting Go*

. . . . . . . . . . .

I decided not to go back to teaching in my pre-K classroom because the start of school would be right about at the end of my recovery period. I would have had to go back into my classroom—and it takes a lot of physical activity to get the room ready and to go on home visits—as well as mentally be there, and I just was not ready. I had gone through not only physical trauma but emotional trauma as well. Often, the scars we cannot see take the longest to heal. I did want to be involved, so in September I agreed to go in a couple of days a week and be the music teacher. This was a wonderful way to keep me involved and have the time I needed to heal.

By October we were back for IVF cycle number two. Insurance would only cover five cycles, and it had a start date and an end date. I had to get pre-authorization for the medicine they wanted to use and the specific therapy they wanted to try. I had to do the treatments in the order the insurance company said. I was required to try one type of treatment before they would approve the next, and the doctors had to show why I would benefit from one treatment as opposed to another. The paperwork involved is tedious and arduous. We now know how this process can take a long time, and the months easily turn into years. It was now almost five years since Colby had been born. It had been three and a half years of trying to conceive, eating organic, doing yoga, taking shots of wheatgrass juice, and then taking shots of GONAL-f, HCG, and Lupron.

I had to consent to these treatments as well, signing a paper saying I understand and will only use barrier contraception during my cycle because it is important not to be pregnant during the cycle when the medicine is used. The long-term effects on the patient and fetus are unknown, but it was being recommended for my next cycle because the doctor felt it could improve my ovulatory response. I also had to sign a paper saying I had read the warning and accepted the risks. Gonadotropin therapy was another treatment used when other methods to achieve pregnancy had failed. It works by stimulating the ovaries to develop multiple eggs. The risks involved include severe hyperstimulation and multiple pregnancies, meaning twins or triplets. And, as with pretty much anything, there is the risk of unexpected complications, with no guarantees or promises.

I knew I should be grateful that I had this opportunity, that my insurance covered the expenses—and I was. But I was also scared. Scared of the drugs and scared of not taking the drugs. Afraid of taking them, while at the same time afraid that, if I do not take them, I will not be able to have another baby. At the same time, I was also going to an acupuncturist. Acupuncture has been noted to help with fertility. It can help regulate hormone function, increase blood flow to the ovaries and uterus, and help relax your body in general, which can improve the chances of the embryo implanting and lower stress levels. My acupuncturist was also like a therapist. She would listen to my concerns and always had tips to tune into my well-being. She became my confidant and healer. She could feel my energy and move it. I loved going to her, and she inspired me to follow my own path and stay true to my inner being. She became an integral part of my journey.

There were other steps I took to reduce stress as well. I stopped watching the news years ago, and I also watched mostly comedies to help my general well-being. I was not kidding earlier when I said laughter is the best medicine. Laughter triggers the production of endorphins in the brain, which makes you feel good, relaxes your blood vessels, and reduces tension by increasing blood flow. Laughter definitely helps counteract the stress of all the scheduling and timing of all the intricate details when using a team of professionals to conceive a baby!

On October 15, 2006, because of the gonadotropin therapy, I had twelve oocytes retrieved. An oocyte is just a fancy word for an immature egg. The oocyte in a "normal" pregnancy will eventually travel down the fallopian tube, at which time it is then called an egg. For all intents and purposes, from here on, I will just refer to these as eggs. They then used my husband's sperm to fertilize the best ones. We had three embryos selected for transfer. Three days later, on October 18, under the use of transabdominal ultrasound and a catheter, the three embryos were transferred into a depth of five centimeters in my uterus. Everything went well, and hopefully, within ten days or so, we would be pregnant. Unfortunately, none took this time. We would wait, let my body recover, and try again.

The discussion of selective reduction came up. I forget who started it, but the thought of this was a very touchy subject. For those who do not know, selective reduction is the process in which you reduce the pregnancy for a more viable healthy outcome. The risks with a multiple birth increase significantly with three or more fetuses. There was a part of me that thought I would be fine to carry multiples because my second son had been so large. If I could carry a nine pound twelve ounce, twenty-two-inch singleton, I figured my body could probably handle multiples. I felt like my issue was not carrying the pregnancy but conceiving it. I knew we were using science to create the embryos and could be causing situations that might not happen naturally otherwise. With this comes unwanted situations, riskier situations, and potentially life-threatening situations for both the mom and the babies.

After going through the tubal and all the heartache that went with that, it was a devastating prospect to have to think about selective reduction. *What if I were to get pregnant with multiples? Could my body handle it? Would it be safe for them and me? Would I be able to selectively reduce if it were suggested by the doctors as the safest thing to do?* I honestly did not feel like I could. After losing a pregnancy, whether it is spontaneous abortion, tubular, miscarriage, or anything, once you have lost a pregnancy or are unable to continue with it for any reason, you are no longer the same person. It changes you, and you feel a real loss. Some people might say, "Well, it was a blighted ovum with no actual fetus, or you miscarried early, so it means it was not meant to be." Bullshit! If you have never been a pregnant woman who, for any reason, could not continue her pregnancy, then you have no idea how hard this decision is. I never wanted to feel this loss again. However, after every unsuccessful cycle, I felt a real loss, even though I was technically not pregnant. We were making embryos, and each one had the potential to be a human being. Not being able to give that potential a chance at life is the worst feeling imaginable!

On March 4, 2007, we were back for IVF cycle number three and egg retrieval day. They were able to retrieve five eggs this time. Three days later, we had two embryos selected and ready for transfer. Once again, everything went great and exactly as planned. We got the call, and once again, unfortunately, it had not produced the outcome we had been looking for. No pregnancy.

Next, June 20, 2007, was IVF cycle number four's egg retrieval day. They were able to get nine eggs this time. They fertilized and created four embryos. They selected all four embryos to be implanted. I was on the hospital bed, ready to go in, and I started having a panic attack; I as literally crying. The doctor was confused, and she asked me why I was crying. Shouldn't this be a good thing? I was starting to realize that if I get pregnant with quadruplets, we could have six kids. Not to mention the risks associated with multiple births, and the possibility of selective reduction. I did not want to deal with any of these scenarios. Some people have six or more kids unassisted and welcome having these big families. We wanted one more child, I would have even loved it if it turned out to be twins, but the idea of that many total children and multiples was overwhelming to me. I was also starting to think this has got to work. The chances of at least one implantation goes up with putting multiple embryos in.

We told the doctor we have two children at home already, and she made a joke, saying now she understood why I was crying. We had to have faith that we would only get what we could handle. We told them to go ahead with the transfer. On June 23, the doctor placed four embryos to the depth of 5.25 centimeters into my uterus. I was excited and nervous at the same time. On the drive home, with my feet up on the dashboard to give them a little extra help from gravity, I looked at my husband with pools of tears in my eyes and said, "I feel like I'm praying for one of them not to make it, and it feels awful!"

Paul so very calmly looked at me and said, "No, you are praying that one of them does make it!" It was one of those amazing moments when I realized how to flip my perspective to what I *do* want, and away from what I *do not* want. He just did this naturally in that moment of panic and was the even keel I needed to steer myself back onto course. Yes, he was completely right. I had to start praying that one of them would make it, and that is exactly what I did. We waited for the call. Once again, there was no pregnancy.

I did not understand. Why was I having this strong desire if I was not supposed to have another child? Was there another message saying to stop, and I was not hearing it? I mentioned to my acupuncturist at a session that I had been questioning our decision to keep going. Maybe it was time to stop. But if that was the case, then why did I not feel complete? The only way I can describe it is that my desire was calling *me*. I was not going out looking for it. I felt my intuition and my instincts were saying that I was supposed to have another child. And I believe my intuition is infinite intelligence, or Spirit, or the universe, or God. I always felt I would have a girl, but this went way beyond that. Sure, that was part of it, but it was just the unknown. The unknown of the possibility of the next child, girl or boy. I also did not want to feel defeated. I wanted to say when, not from frustration or fear, but because I knew it was time. Because I knew my family was complete. And I just did not feel that yet. I told my acupuncturist there was a part of me that thought this was not God or Spirit testing me to see how badly I wanted it, but rather a desire that came from Spirit, not from me to Spirit, but the other way around, from Spirit to me. If you have ever had an inner calling, you will know what I'm talking about. It is a knowing before you can possibly know. It is a feeling that is calling to you. It is not a willful or demanding feeling, but a visceral, allover, from-the-core-of-your-being feeling, and you are being pulled in the direction of it. So why was it not happening?

During my next cycle I was having a very prolonged period. I had a history of an ectopic pregnancy that also showed chronic salpingitis, which basically meant my fallopian tube was inflamed. I had not gotten pregnant after four IVF cycles with a transfer of "very nice embryos," according to the doctor's notes. For these reasons, she scheduled an endometrial biopsy to evaluate my uterine lining and to rule out chronic endometritis, and as a possible explanation for my prolonged period and lack of implantation of embryos. This test showed I had a normal uterine cavity and tubal ostia, which meant my tube was open at the end, like it should be. Everything was normal.

It was October 2, 2007, and IVF cycle number five, egg retrieval day. The doctor was able to retrieve seven eggs from this cycle. We waited to hear how many embryos we would have. There was one embryo hatched—number four—and it was selected for transfer. We waited for the call, and once again, it was negative, no pregnancy. We were scheduled for a follow-up with the doctor to discuss our options moving forward.

The meeting took place at the IVF clinic in the doctor's office. I honestly cannot remember what options she gave us, primarily because I think our minds were made up at this point. I could not do it anymore. I had all these drugs in my body, and I felt an internal conflict because I was trying to be so healthy. I was putting only organic, warm foods in my body. I was drinking wheatgrass juice. I was doing yoga. I was doing acupuncture. I was drinking tea, and not coffee. I did not use the microwave. I used only pads when I got my period, no tampons. I was not drinking alcohol. I did not watch the news. We watched funny movies. I used visualizations to make my womb a warm, nice place an embryo would like to go to. We went on vacations, and we tried to forget about it and let it happen. We had done multiple rounds of IUIs, and we had done multiple rounds of IVF. I had read so many books and had such hope. I had to let go for now. I just had one question for the doctor: could I still physically conceive naturally?

She responded by telling me that my eggs were old and dark in color. So we asked what that meant. The doctor told us that it did not necessarily mean anything. We were confused. She explained more. These were the physical characteristics of the eggs, but there was no proof that it meant anything was wrong with them, or an indicator of anything exactly. These characteristics did *not* correlate to the viability of the eggs.

My husband then said jokingly, "So let me get this straight. You're telling us these are the characteristics, but they have no bearing on the outcome of a healthy pregnancy? So it does not mean we will give birth to a five-year-old, dark-skinned child?" He was being funny because she had said my eggs were chronologically old and were dark in color. We both started laughing. My husband is a quiet person but has a knack for saying something funny at the right time to break the tension.

So, if these characteristics do not mean anything, then why was the doctor pointing them out? We did not understand. Was she trying to scare us? I knew I was getting up there in maternal age. I was thirty-eight now, so could this mean I was at a greater risk of having a child with a birth defect or risk to my health? Many women older than me have healthy babies every day.

Finally, I looked her in the eyes and said, "Can you just tell me if I can physically have another baby? I now only have one fallopian tube; will this affect my chances?"

She reassured me that the fallopian tube is like an arm that will reach out and get the egg, no matter which side it is on. So, no, that would not be an issue.

I said again, "So I can conceive physically? There's no physical reason I couldn't conceive naturally at home?"

My doctor took a deep breath and sighed. She then looked me directly in the eyes and said, "Well, crazier things have happened!"

Yes, indeed, crazier things have happened. I thought, *OK, well, that's all I need to know!* I just needed to know it could still happen physically. We thanked her and said we were going to take a break over the holidays and decide if we wanted to do anything further after the new year.

I decided that I needed to go home and be with my boys. I could not be this emotional roller coaster of a person and be a good mom. I had to stop the drugs. My body had either been pregnant or on fertility meds, so it had thought it was pregnant for the better part of the last ten years. I needed to be happy. I needed to go have fun with my kids again. I needed to let this go. I needed to let go of the thought that something was wrong with me. I needed to stop trying to fix it. I had to start with the only thing I could control—and that was me, my thoughts, my emotions, and my actions. If I could not have another baby, there was nothing I could do about it.

There were other options. Maybe we would consider adoption? Maybe it would just be us and our two boys, and I was happy with that. I stopped letting something outside of me dictate my emotions. I stopped letting circumstances I had no control over determine my attitude and outlook on life. I remember distinctly thinking, *My boys deserve a happy, healthy mom, physically and mentally!* Now that, I could control. I had to, as they say, give this up to God. I had to let go and let God. I knew Spirit had given me the desire for another child. Maybe the path to him or her was just something else, another way I had not considered yet. I was scared to let go. I had focused on this for the better part of ten years. My focus had been on becoming a mom. Now I had to switch my focus to *being* a mom. I was always there for my boys, and I was a very attentive and involved parent. I was being the best me I knew how, but now I would become more mentally present with them and with my husband.

It was a huge weight lifted off my shoulders. You do not realize when you are living it every day what a toll this diagnosis of infertility can take on you. It was time to get happy for my boys, for my husband, and for myself. Could I let go of this dream and be happy? What if it never happened? Because that was the reality of it. And my answer was a resounding, *Hell yes!* Of course I could. I already was happy; that wasn't the question for me. My inner struggle became about why I was feeling this pull. Why had I gone through all of this if the outcome had not changed? What difference had this all made? Except now I knew the pain of losing another unborn baby, but this time, one who had been a live pregnancy. I now had only one fallopian tube. Why would I be put back in the position I had been in to begin with, only now with less equipment for the job? It did not make sense to me. How could I have been so wrong about this inner feeling? I decided that letting go did not have to mean letting go of this desire. Letting go could just mean letting go of trying to make it happen. Letting go of trying so hard, of pushing against. I could let go of the struggle, but not the desire.

So I focused on the only thing I could. I focused on my family. We had a wonderful holiday season. We relaxed and enjoyed the company of friends and family. After the holidays, I joined a gym with the boys. They loved going there to swim and play basketball, and they often brought a friend. I tried different types of yoga classes and even had some sessions with a personal trainer. It was going to be a great new year. I put my thoughts about another baby in the back of my mind. I was not denying my thoughts, just sitting with them for now. I stopped focusing on what was not working and focused on what was working. I had two beautiful boys and a wonderful husband. I was truly blessed. I knew I had come close to losing them, and I had risked my life. I had gone back after the cyst removal and done more IVF cycles, which I knew was not a popular decision among many family members. However, I had my truth, and I knew what it was.

This was my decision; mine, and Paul's. He had been scared, too, but he wanted me to follow my heart's desire as much as I did. I told myself, if it's meant to be, it will happen. I did not say I did not want it anymore. I knew I still wanted it, but not at this cost. Could I have it all? Could I let it go and not make myself crazy? Gratitude was my answer. I reminded myself every day of all the things I had to be grateful for, and in doing so, my life became about the blessings of life.

Colby had been born the November after the September 11 attack. I remember being pregnant with him, and Joe being so little, when that horror rocked our world. But we survived, we moved on, and we had so much to be grateful and thankful for. Out of that tragedy, so many stories of people helping each other and being genuinely kind humans were told. The legacy of September 11 was the humanity that was shown to strangers in a time of need, and how many selfless acts of kindness were revealed. Life is truly a precious gift! I always told Joe he had been given to me twice: once at birth, and once again when he survived his illness. What a gift! I now had to remind myself that I had been given life twice as well: when my mom gave birth to me, and when my baby gave its life for mine. Yes, life is a precious gift meant to be enjoyed every day, not to be taken for granted. And now was the time for me to remind myself how beautiful and blessed this life is, for me and for my beautiful family.

"You don't learn
how strong you are
until you are pushed
beyond what you
thought you could handle
and you emerge on
the other side
with more bravery,
grace and determination
than you realized
you ever had."
—Rachel Marie Martin

## CHAPTER 10

# *Am I on a Hidden Camera Show?*

. . . . . . . . .

It was now February, and the gym was a great escape from the cold, New England weather outside. We could go swimming and play basketball and pretend we were somewhere warm. Sometimes I would go without the boys and take a hot yoga class or do sessions with the personal trainer. I had been going for a few weeks now, and I did sessions with the trainer once a week, then the exercises on my own for the week. It was like a weekly check-in trainer session. I noticed I did not feel like I was losing any weight after a few weeks in. I felt kind of tired and bloated, and I realized it was probably because my period was about to start. I asked the trainer about it, and she said I could have gained some water weight because, at the beginning of starting to exercise again, this could happen. I figured that, along with my PMS, was definitely contributing to my bloating and fatigue.

Over the next week, I realized that it was my twenty-eighth day and no period had started. *OK, relax,* I said to myself. *Give it a couple of days.* Whenever I get pregnant, I always have two definite signs. First, I do not get a pimple or two, which I do get every month before my period. Second, my boobs ache. And I had both! I waited until day thirty, and although this was still early, since I was exercising, I wanted to make sure I did not do anything to jeopardize a pregnancy.

It was a Saturday morning, and I decided, what the heck, I'll do an early pregnancy test. If I am pregnant, it will show because it's day thirty. After I had done so many, I did not have an optimistic feeling about it. Even though I had my two definitive signs, I still doubted myself. I waited and set my timer. *It's probably going to be negative anyway*, I thought. I walked out of the bathroom and left the test on the sink as I waited. The timer went off, and just as I opened the door to go back into the bathroom, a little voice inside my head said, *Yeah, but what if it's not negative this time?* It was a split second, a block of thought, not necessarily word for word, but just more of a feeling.

I looked at the test, and it had two lines. Two distinct lines. Not one light and one dark. Not a maybe. But two solid, blue lines. *Oh my God! Is this really happening?* I started screaming, and I called to Paul. Of course, the boys were wondering what was going on. And I quickly made up something to tell them. Paul came in and saw it, too. It wasn't just me; I wasn't seeing things that weren't there. We were ecstatic.

I said to Paul, "Did we even have sex this month? I honestly don't remember." We started laughing and could not believe this was happening. Crazier things have happened, alright! However, this was definitely at the top of our list.

The next day was Sunday, and we would usually go to church as a family. The boys had a Sunday school class before the actual church service, and I was also taking an adult educational class. As I was not raised in a church, I enjoyed getting to know more about the Bible, and things that a lot of people just know but I did not. Paul was raised Catholic, so he would usually get a coffee or do something and then come back when the church service was about to start. I was running late, as usual, and went to the library where the class I had been taking was usually held. However, for some reason, on that day, the places where the classes were being held got switched around. As I was late, I had not heard the announcement of the classes moving locations. So I proceeded to the library. I sort of snuck in, sat down, and looked around. I noticed these were not the same people who had been in my class last week. I was not the best at paying attention to these things, and I figured maybe we had started a new class or something, and I just was not aware of it. Eventually, I asked the lady next to me, and she said it was a different class. As I was already late, I figured, what the heck, I would just stay here and learn something different that I did not know about.

The class was about poetry as prayer. The class syllabus showed the class had started the week prior. You were supposed to read the poem for the coming week once a day for the week leading up to the class. I obviously had not had the materials or anything, so they just handed me the packet of mimeographed pages. They were happy to have another person in the group, it did not matter to them that I was jumping in. That day was February 17, and the selection for the day was Psalms 139:13–18. Now, remember, I was the only one in this room who knew I was pregnant, and I was only one of two people (Paul being the other) in the entire universe who knew this fact. The psalm reads as follows:

"For it was you who formed my inward parts;
You knit me together in my mother's womb."
(I slowly looked around, like, how does someone else know this?)
"I praise you, for I am fearfully and wonderfully made.
Wonderful are your works;
That I know very well.
My frame was not hidden from you,
When I was being made in secret,"
(OK, how does someone know my secret? This is not like Paul to pull a practical joke of this nature. This baby was totally made in secret because we did not even remember the conception. I felt like God was working behind the scenes."
"Intricately woven in the depths of the earth.
Your eyes beheld my unformed substance."
(Holy crap, this means God, or Spirit, knows! Spirit knows I am pregnant and is telling me it's going to be OK. Is this really happening right now? Spirit sees the unformed substance of my baby.)
"In your book were written all the days that were formed for me,
When none of them as yet existed."
(It is said that God knows all the days that your life is going to be, that they are known before your birth. I have heard this before, and now, somehow, through this poem, I am getting a message directly from Spirit.)
"How weighty to me are your thoughts, O God!
How vast is the sum of them!
I try to count them—they are more than the sand;
I come to the end—I am still with you."
This section let me know that Spirit knew what I was thinking. And Spirit was thinking about me and my baby as well. That there are too many

thoughts to count, more than the sand. And that, through all of this, Spirit had been with me and would continue to be with me and my child until the end. And that Spirit was also with my babies. That Spirit knew each and every one of them from before they were even formed into substance in my womb, or, in some instances, formed in the test tube and then put into my womb.

I needed a tissue; I was overcome with emotions. I felt a sense of calm and reassurance, like nothing I had ever felt before. A quiet and serene confidence fell over me. I knew everything I had gone through had been worth it because it had brought me to this moment. This moment of knowing. This moment of knowing this pregnancy was going to last. This moment of knowing that it had all been for a reason. That none of it had been a mistake. That it was all for me. For me to know how it all works, and why. I knew this time I was going to get the outcome I had so desired all this time. And it was not because I had tried for so long or because I was now more deserving than before, but because this time I had let go and trusted myself and my inner being and followed my heart and just loved. I loved my life. I loved my husband. I loved my family. And I had let go and allowed Spirit to move through me.

I honestly felt like I was on a hidden camera show, like someone was going to pop out from behind the door and say, "Smile! You're on *Candid Camera*!" But I knew I could not be. I was on "spiritual" *Candid Camera*. There was this message being given to me in fairly plain language. The Bible is always open to interpretation, but there was no denying the message of this passage. This was the biggest "God wink" or "spiritual nod" I had ever received. And it was so plainly obvious to me. I still get goose bumps when I think about that day and how it was so synchronistic. All the little details had lined up. There was also a bigger message that I would come to understand later. That it's all good! Everything happens for a reason. Even the most seemingly devastating events can lead to good things. It is all good! Life is all good!

I had to stop going to the gym. I had to be careful with this pregnancy, the doctor told me. My OB is an amazing woman, whom I love deeply. She is one of the kindest, warmhearted, and loveliest people I will ever know. She had done the D&C way back when, she had been there for my entire pregnancy with Colby, and she was there for this entire pregnancy.

They did an ultrasound, and everything looked great. I never even had any spotting with this pregnancy. At the appropriate gestational age, they asked if we wanted to know which sex the baby was. We said yes. I had mixed feelings, but they were all good! I would, on the one hand, love to have a girl, just because I had not gotten to experience that yet. But, on the other hand, now that he or she was going to be seven and twelve years younger than his or her older brothers, I thought it would be nice if it was a boy. I felt they would have more things to bond over. I knew that, no matter what, they would all love each other, and it was all good. A healthy pregnancy and a healthy baby were what was important.

The ultrasound tech came in. She put the jelly on my belly and asked again if we wanted to know. Yes, please, we have literally been waiting forever. *It's a boy!* I had tears in my eyes, but they were tears of relief. I had thought all along that a girl would be nice, but when she said it was a boy, a wave of comfort and relief came over me. I was simply happy to be having a healthy baby, and I totally knew what to do with a boy. We had this! I knew it was all good! Well, unbeknownst to us, the surprises were not over yet. The rest of the pregnancy went along unremarkably, as they say. I always loved being pregnant. It is an amazing feeling, to know life is growing inside of you, knowing that you've made a new life.

Knowing that this was going to be our last child, and my mom's last grandchild, I invited her to be in the delivery room. My mom and I were awfully close. As with most mother-daughter relationships, we've had some rocky moments, but we've always remained best friends in the end. She was over-the-moon excited to be able to witness the birth. When she'd had my brother in 1967 and myself in 1969, the birth plan had been more like, we will knock you out, and when you wake up, you'll have a beautiful baby in your arms. Not much active involvement, even though it was all coming from her. Paul was totally OK with this—well, maybe not totally, but he went along with it anyway. He understood how much it meant to both of us, and being the kindhearted, lovable guy that he is, he agreed.

We had made a plan to test from the umbilical cord sample again to check for the metabolic disorder. It was the same as we had done seven years earlier with Colby. It was getting close to my due date, and I went into the office for my check up, and they sent me directly from there to the hospital. I had started to dilate; it was time. Since I'd had the epidural with the gallbladder/cyst surgery, and everything had been fine, I decided that I would have one this time. I was older and wiser at this point. The nurses reassured me that I would still feel everything, so I would know when to push, but it was sort of like a numbing effect. They said it would just take the edge off the pain. That sounded like a good plan to me. I was no longer deathly afraid of needles, like I had been twelve and seven years earlier. I'd had enough needles poked and prodded into me that it was no longer an issue. With all the IVF cycles, the tests, and the surgeries, I was good with needles now.

Before I got to the point where they would do the epidural, I would find a focal point in the room and do my breathing to get through the contractions. They waited to try to time the epidural so that it would numb at the right time, at the contractions right before and when you have to push. I decided that the clock just in front of me on the wall at the end of the bed was a good place to focus. Paul and my mom were in the room with me. We had walked around the floor a few times, and the contractions were coming on a bit now. I felt one coming on, and when I went to look at my focal point, my mom was standing directly in front of it so I could not see it. Through my concentrated, labored breathing, I said, "Mom, move!" and waved my hand to signal her out of my way.

She looked at me and asked, "Why? What are you talking about? I'm just standing here. Why should I move?"

I thought, *I cannot believe her right now. She has no clue that she is standing directly in my line of sight and blocking my focal point. I obviously cannot argue with her at this point because I'm trying my damnedest to just breathe.*

After that contraction subsided, I said, "Mom, do me a favor. When a woman in labor asks you to move, just do it! You were standing in front of my focal point as I was trying to breathe."

She replied, "Oh, sorry, I didn't realize. I was wondering why you needed me to move. Why didn't you just say so?" Um, because I couldn't breathe, never mind talk to her and explain why. This was so her! They made everyone leave the room so they could put the epidural in. When my mom was allowed back in the room, she made sure not to block my focal point again.

They put monitors on the baby throughout the labor. His heartbeat was a little wacky. The nurses always make jokes and try to make you feel less concerned. The one nurse was dancing around the room to the baby's heartbeat, saying, "You can dance the cha-cha to this one." They told me it happens sometimes, and it's nothing to be super concerned with. Of course, I knew the drill by this time, and I was a little concerned.

They placed the monitor on the baby's scalp while he was still in my womb. They were right, I could still feel the contractions, but just with not as much intensity. Once he was through the birth canal, they took him. I was concerned and nervous. Was he OK? What was going on? There had been no indications of an issue with his heart from earlier ultrasounds throughout the pregnancy. Maybe it was the epidural … that could slow it down. But his heart was doing the cha-cha? It was beating irregularly.

They took him under the heat lamp and examined him. His heart rate calmed down and was now in a more natural rhythm.

Mom said to me, "I think he has red hair."

As she had held one leg and my husband held the other, I had no doubt she thought she knew what she saw. What I was questioning was her reasoning behind this determination. I told her that it was just his head. His scalp was red from the birthing process, along with his entire body, which was a nice, bright pink color.

She said, "No, I think it's his hair."

Sure enough, I had to eat my words. Baby Garret's hair was a strawberry blonde. He was beautiful! Nine pounds eight ounces, and 21.25 inches long, he was a perfect mix of his brothers. Oh, and yes, he, too, had amazingly beautiful blue eyes!

This was the other surprise that had been kept secret from us, the color of his hair. Joe had been born with a full head of dark hair that had fallen out in clumps and grew back in blonde; and Colby had literally been born with frosted tips, the ends of his hair were blonde, and he was very blonde as a child. I felt like this was another sign from Spirit, as none of us had even thought of this. Paul and I had dirty blonde hair, and none of our siblings had red hair, none of our parents did, and none of our nieces and nephews did. We did, however, both have cousins with red hair. His cousins' had more of a bright red, and my one cousin has that pretty auburn color. But Garret's hair was strawberry blonde, and he had blue eyes. One of his eyes also had a brown section in it. He was unique.

He was definitely "fearfully and wonderfully made." This does not mean afraid or scared, but instead, "fearfully," when translated from Hebrew, means with great reverence, heartfelt interest, and with respect. "Wonderfully," when translated from Hebrew, means unique and set apart. When I read this, it reaffirmed that Psalms 139:13–18 was indeed a specific message to me about Garret. That he was created with great reverence, heartfelt interest, and respect to be unique and set apart, as we all are. But, in this case, even more so because of all the circumstances surrounding his miraculous conception and birth, and that he is truly a gift from Spirit. If you know his personality, it even reinforces this more. Garret is undeniably fearfully and wonderfully made.

## CHAPTER 11

# Life with Boys

. . . . . . . . .

I distinctly remember having a sigh of relief after Garret was born. While I am not sure if I said it audibly or just in my head, I clearly recall thinking, *OK, what now?* I had done it. We had done it! We had our family, our beautiful party of five. We had beaten all the crazy odds, not through determination, but by faith. By letting go and being happy and just saying, "Whatever it'll be, it'll be!" We had allowed the miracle of life to flow easily into our lives. I was only briefly concerned when they noticed his crazy cha-cha heartbeat. They did not know what I knew. They had not gotten that amazing wink I had gotten from the poem, telling me directly that Source or Spirit was on the case! I honestly knew that nothing was going to be wrong with him. I never even questioned it.

It was determined that Garret had one kidney larger than the other, and there was a concern for possible hydronephrosis, which is when one kidney is larger than the other, which can cause urination issues and infections. However, he never had any symptoms or issues at all, and by the time he was four or five, the doctor and I agreed that even though ultrasounds are an amazing diagnostic tool, they also show us things that we would never even know were there. In this case, his one kidney was slightly larger than the other but it was a completely benign issue. It was a characteristic that many people probably walk around with and never even realize. And, as far as the metabolic disorder, we knew what to do now to keep them all safe. It was more of a formality for them to tell me if he had it or not. I'd had children with it for twelve years now, so I could handle it, no matter what.

Having children with an extremely rare metabolic disorder inherently presents itself with some challenges. Like trying to explain it to other medical professionals who have no idea what you are talking about. The first time Joe ever got sick was when we were still living down the Cape. He had an ear infection and had to take the pink medicine, amoxicillin. He had also just had a strawberry-pink yogurt tube when he vomited for the first time since being home from recovering from his illness. In hindsight, I think it was like a mouthful, but being in hypersensitive mode at the time from almost losing him, I was freaked out. Plus, this had been the first time we had to deal with knowing he needed outside energy sources, and we were super vigilant about it. We did not know if he was going to keep vomiting or what. We were incredibly nervous, to say the least. So we had to take him to the local hospital. I think we even called the ambulance!

When we got there, the hospital was rather vacant. My grandmother later told me that it was the oldest hospital on the Cape, and they had gone there when they used to live in New Jersey and my dad was a kid, but they'd summered here on the Cape. It did not surprise me, it looked like it was that old! The nurse came in and grabbed a paper towel from the dispenser on the wall to take notes on. I looked at my husband with my eye-rolling face like, *Oh, hell no! She is not seriously going to take notes about my child on a goddamned paper towel! Can't they afford a notepad, for crying out loud?* We then proceeded to explain his medical situation about the ear infection and his metabolic disorder, and the nurse and the doctor looked at each other, both females, and one of them said, "Who thought this one up?" (Referring to the metabolic disorder diagnosis.) She said it out the side of her mouth but in an audible tone. We were like, "Um, we can hear you!"

We then quietly discussed with each other, so they could not hear us, how we could just scoop Joe up and run for it. We could get to our hospital, back in Weymouth, and back in this century, in about forty-five minutes! The hospital staff eventually did what was needed, giving him antibiotics through his IV so he would not have to take the amoxicillin again. This would get rid of his ear infection, and since we did not know if he had thrown up from the temperature or from an allergic reaction to the medicine (since his vomit had been pink, and he'd had the pink yogurt), this would take care of the situation. We then left with our son, said thank you, and vowed never to go back there again!

Over the years, with three boys, we have had many trips to the doctor and the hospital. Paul is accident-prone, and I am klutzy. Perhaps we should have thought more about these genes than the metabolic disorder before having children? I grew up with my brother, just one boy, and he and his friends were always doing something to get hurt. Paul and his brother could write their own book on the crazy shenanigans they got into. Our boys definitely inherited their dad's, and perhaps the "boy" gene, for (how can I put this delicately?) being an idiot, doing stupid boy things, breaking bones, getting injured, having dumb luck, being adventurous with no fear, and thinking it was fun! It was fun—to them!

Their primary care doctor gave me some good advice after the diagnosis. She gently reminded me that they would still get normal sicknesses. They would get colds and strep throat, have ear infections, injuries, and perhaps allergies, etc. Not everything would be a metabolic crisis. I clearly had PTSD from the experience with Joe, and I was a tad hyper about anything that happened with my boys. I will always be grateful to her for keeping me calm and giving me a steady, rational perspective when I needed it!

One of the biggest challenges we faced over the years with children who have a rare metabolic disorder was when one of them would get a stomach bug. The first few times with Joe, we rushed to the hospital. We had an ER doctor call our metabolic doctor once when we were in the ER with Joe, and she let us know that he suggested we had an hour or so to get him to the hospital when this happened. I was like, "OK, well, we live at least half an hour away without traffic, so how about I leave right away to get here because that is what makes me feel comfortable. No harm done, right?"

We kind of got used to medical professionals trying to tell us what to do. They could not understand how nonmedical people understood something they did not. We had our share of doctors and nurses who did not follow our instructions about the 10-percent dextrose IV, even with a protocol letter from the metabolic doctor. We learned very quickly to advocate for ourselves and our children. I cannot count the number of times when, after I've explained the disorder, I would be asked if I was in the medical field. "Um, no, I am the parent of a child who has a rare condition, and we live with it every day, so I know how it works!"

Even though it is called an unspecified FOD, they still know how to handle it. The treatment is the same. Whether or not we have a specific name attached to it does not matter. We had some young ER doctors try to change our protocol, like they were going to come up with something better than the genetic/metabolic specialist with thirty years' experience. I do not think so! I would have to ask politely to please just follow the protocol letter, and if they had any questions, to call the metabolic doctor on call at Boston Children's Hospital because they all know what to do! The stomach bugs were the hardest when they were babies because we knew if the vomiting were to be continuous, they would have to go and get IVs; and after the first time, they got wise to this, and they obviously did not want to go. But, as they got older, we could wait and see if they could eat or drink after a few hours. Joe always seemed to have the hardest time with this. Even in high school. Once, he just could not keep anything down. It had been a few hours, and eventually he conceded that it was not going away.

It is amazing how he will not feel well, and then he'll get sick, the dehydration starts to kick in, he feels nauseated, and it becomes this cyclical downward spiral, and I can actually see him getting worse. After he gets the proper IV, it is amazing how quickly he will start to bounce back. You can actually witness his lethargy lift and his energy come back to him. Colby has always had a rock gut, and even from a much younger age, if he woke up and got sick twice, I would let him go back to sleep, and he would wake up and have Popsicles for breakfast and be fine.

Another bad one was strep throat for us. If we got it in time, they could be fine. Once, when Colby was in pre-K, he was eating lime tortilla chips when I got the call that the test was positive. I was like, "Are you sure? 'Cause he's eating lime tortilla chips, and his throat is not bothering him at all." Yup! I also do not think my boys feel pain like other people do. They have extremely high thresholds for pain. Another time, Colby got scarlet fever because he had shown no strep symptoms at all, and all of a sudden, he had this rash all over his body. I felt like a bad mom because scarlet fever only happens if you do not catch the fact that the person has strep, but I knew I had not done anything wrong.

Once, with Garret, we went to the ER because he had a fever and just kept vomiting. They tested for strep, and it was positive, so they were like, "OK, we have an answer. Here is your medicine. You can go home." We got off the highway, and he vomited all over the back seat of the car. Even though they had discovered the reason for the vomiting, they still needed to keep him with IVs until he could keep food and drink down. We drove home, cleaned him up, wiped the car down as best we could, and turned right around and drove back. And they had to admit him overnight. He needed to get the hydration and dextrose from the IV before his body could begin to heal. It was not until he had that, and they'd put antibiotics for the strep in his IV, that he finally felt better.

We have had an above-average number of broken bones, surgeries, concussions, stitches, and bumps and bruises in the last twenty-four years of parenthood. This included the time when they thought Colby needed an appendectomy. Our metabolic doctor had moved to Tufts Medical Center. We were sent there so he could oversee Colby's treatment. The first ultrasound tech said it was an inflamed appendix, and it looked like he might have to have it removed, so they sent us by ambulance into Boston. They kept him, with me on the chairbed, overnight to observe and reassess in the morning. During the night, an attending doctor—who did not understand Colby's metabolic disorder—saw the IV written for 10% dextrose solution or D10 and changed it to D5. As I was half asleep, I heard the nurse changing the IV bag. I was groggy and thought maybe it ran out.

I got up, checked the bag, and I was so pissed. I asked the nurse to change it back. She explained that, because a doctor had written to change it, she could not just change it back. So I thought, *Fine, I'll take care of it!* And I called our metabolic doctor on my cell. He then called in to the doctor who was on staff and instructed him to change it back to D10. Problem solved.

I have learned to advocate for my child, even when that means questioning a doctor. When something isn't right to me, I question until I hear what's being said, and then I feel in my own heart if it resonates with me. Every person is unique, and every situation is unique, and it always needs to sound reasonable to me. Since we had first gone into the ER with his stomach pains the day before, Colby had not had anything to eat or drink for quite a long time. In case they had to operate, he was not allowed to eat or drink anything. This was why I pushed so hard for the D10. I knew it had been a significant amount of time without intakes, and I felt he was not safe on a D5. There have been other situations in which my child was scheduled for the first procedure in the morning where they do not even put them on a D10 IV because it's really no longer fasting than it would be overnight. I'm OK with that, I understand that. This, however, was a doctor not understanding the condition, and instead of asking questions, he just changed things. That was not OK, and I knew it, and I'm glad I have learned to speak up.

I had prayed on our ambulance ride into town that Colby would get the best doctor for him. Not that he did not have to have an appendectomy or that he would not have an operation, but that what was best for him would happen. I did not want to pray for no operation if that was what was needed. I did not want to pray for a successful operation if he did not necessarily need one. Since it was not a clear, definitive thing, I just prayed for the best possible outcome for my child.

They ended up checking a stress marker in the blood that actually showed that he did not have to have surgery. I am not sure what the first doctor saw, but we were told that the dye they used to see his abdomen more clearly with medical diagnostic testing also could have resolved it. And since the blood work showed no acute distress, it looked like this had been a false alarm, and he did not have to have surgery.

My friend works in the ER at the first hospital. She has been an ER nurse for twenty years and had been on duty when we had been sent into Boston. She was surprised when we saw her next and said he did not have to have surgery. So what was it? Why did one tech see appendicitis? How did it just go away? I have learned to just say thank you sometimes, and to not let my curiosity get the better of me. It was clearly not nothing, but whatever it was, it was no longer an issue. And the doctor who ended up in charge of his case was definitely the best doctor for him.

Perhaps the hardest thing about being the mom to my three boys has been the injuries. One of the absolute hardest things, as a mom, is to see your child suffering and not be able to fix it for them. When they are little, you can usually kiss away the pain, slap a Band-Aid on, and they'll forget all about what had been bothering them. As they get older, they have older-people problems, and no matter how old they get, they never stop being your child.

When he was in about seventh grade, Joe played football. I had been strongly against this, but I also was adamant about not letting the metabolic disorder dictate my kids' lives. I would not allow it to define them or what they could or could not do. But, to the best of my ability, I would keep them safe! He ended up getting a concussion with cervical spine damage in his neck. He had to have months of physical therapy. During this time, he also had to get stitches over his eye after an accident while making a catapult with his brother. It then got infected, and he had to have IV antibiotics overnight in the hospital. He broke his ankle, but it was misdiagnosed for two weeks, and he walked around on it until he could not anymore. He then developed reflex sympathetic dystrophy (RSD) in his foot, a nerve damage issue with his foot where it would swell up and turn purple because the nerves were misfiring and sending a signal to the brain that it was still damaged. We promptly returned to physical therapy for more treatment.

They fell off their bikes, they flipped off waterslides, they rode their bikes into parked cars, they walked off railroad tie walls, they swung from trees and hit their heads, they broke more ankles, they ran into ladders hanging in the woods behind the neighbor's house while being chased by a pack of coyotes and needed stitches in the head … do not ask! And this is the stuff I know about because they got hurt!

My boys did many things I do not want to know about. Joe even had a heart issue during his senior year of high school. He had to wear a heart monitor and was put on beta-blockers. That messed with his executive function and caused havoc in his senior year. Thankfully, he was planning on going to prep school anyway. We were told it was recommended he have an ablation, which is when they burn or freeze the part of the heart that is misfiring. We said, "Um, second opinion, please!" My friend Lisa, whom I had known for over ten years, and is the mom of Colby's best friend, was a nurse. What I did not know was that she was a cardiac nurse. When she told me this, I said, "Well, of course you are!" Because that is what I needed right then and there. Source provides, and we got our second opinion from an extremely knowledgeable and kind cardiac doctor, the one who my friend worked for. Joe was fine. He had no problem with his heart. In hindsight, I think he was stressed, even though he did not think so, and we had discussed this possibility at the time. He just had not realized it yet, and then getting that diagnosis and thinking he would have to have a heart surgery just added more stress to his life. Yes, life with my boys has definitely been an adventure.

Joe decided to go to prep school so he could get into a better college and give himself a year to get stronger for his sport, baseball. He ended up tearing his ulnar collateral ligament (UCL) at a winter prospect camp down in Florida, and he needed reconstructive surgery, or Tommy John surgery. Because of this, he ended up doing a second year at prep school. This was the best thing for him; he was valedictorian and was awarded multiple awards for baseball, academics, and being a good example of what it means to be a BA wolverine! He learned more about himself and what he was capable of from having this setback than he ever would have had it not occurred. Yes, I would have done anything to take away that pain, but then I would have been robbing him of the growth and self-confidence he gained as he learned to pull himself back up after this adversity. I have never been prouder of him, and as he gave his speech at graduation, I could see in his demeanor that he had never been more confident and prouder of himself, either!

Colby, who has been the starting varsity soccer goalie since he was a freshman, tore the meniscus in his knee the summer before his junior year. He could not play at all that season. All in the same day, he failed his driver's license test and found out he had to have surgery on his knee. It was the worst day of his life! I let him cry for a while because I knew that, no matter what I said at that moment, nothing could make it better for him. When you cannot change the circumstance, you can only change your attitude about it. I then watched over the next few months as he pulled himself up and did whatever he could for his team. He became like a second coach. He showed up to every practice and game, coached the other goalies, was always a positive influence, and cheered on his team. Colby went to physical therapy and got himself better. I was prouder of his attitude and how he handled himself that year than of any amazing save he has ever had in the net. And he has made some pretty impressive saves!

If I could give my children one gift, it would be confidence! Confidence is not about feeling better than or superior to others; that is arrogance.

Confidence is knowing. Confidence is belief. Confidence is understanding. Confidence that everything is always working out for them. Confidence that even in the midst of something unwanted, they are asking for that which is wanted. How would you act, behave, and feel if you knew everything is always working out for you? Would you be more adventurous and try different things? What would you do if you knew you could not fail? Even when something seemingly is not working, or you feel you have failed at something, that does not have to be the end of it.

Every failure is just a lesson learned. Every setback is a tweaking of a wanted desire. There is no failure. It is just a narrowing of focus on what will work now that you know what did not work for you the previous time. Just because it did not work does not mean it cannot work! It just means you need to come at it from a different angle or perspective or belief and see what happens. You must always have confidence. Be confident in yourself, and trust your desires, your feelings, and your abilities to accomplish that which is your heart's truest desire. Be confident that the universe/Source/Spirit already knows your desire and is supporting you or guiding you toward it.

Confidence is trust in yourself. Trust in that which is yet to be because, since it has not happened yet, why not focus on how you would like it to be? Worrying is the opposite of confidence, and it is asking for that which is unwanted by focusing on it. Next time you find yourself daydreaming about all that could go wrong, just stop yourself and think about all the things that could go right! Even when you do not know how, or who, or when, just focus on the feeling of the desired outcome, and the universe must yield it to you! Feel confident that the universe will surround you with others who feel the same and have similar mindsets.

Feel the desired outcome by visualizing it. See it, hear it, smell it, taste it, touch it in your mind's eye. Think about it, dream about it, allow the details to fill in, and know it is already done on an energetic level. Maintain the feeling, and it will be quick to manifest or happen in your physical/material experience. You just have to be confident! And if it's not happening, trust in that too. Trust that it will be, in perfect timing.

CHAPTER 12

# The Love Stone

. . . . . . . . . .

From the moment he was born, Garret shared a unique connection with my mom. She loved all her grandkids fiercely, but there was something about being the baby. Mom had been at his birth, and she'd also helped me take care of him when I was working. She had nicknames for all her grandkids. Dude, Bud, Joe-Stuff, Monkey-Man, Munch, Brades, G-Man, we would go through all this time toiling over the perfect names, and she would destroy them each with her unbridled love. Better her than their siblings, whose nicknames are much worse.

Over the years, Grammy would always be there for school plays, music concerts, and performances. Anything and everything; she was there for all of it, but her favorite was to watch them play sports. They played many of the same sports, but she enjoyed going to watch them all. Whether it was a cold hockey rink in the middle of July, a snowy November soccer game, a brisk spring baseball game, or a lacrosse game in April, she would be there. She was the proudest grammy ever! She also loved taking them to play golf. Golf became a passion of hers in her later years. She loved taking them golfing and teaching them, especially the lefties, because she was a lefty, too. A huge part of her identity revolved around the fact that she was left-handed. She was immensely proud of her left-handedness, and she loved the fact that my brother and I, who are both right-handed, now have kids who are left-handed. She was the only one who could teach them certain left-handed things. After all, as she would so often remind us, "left-handed people are the only ones in their right minds."

In recent years, she developed chronic obstructive pulmonary disease (COPD), which is the stage before emphysema. It is an obstructive lung disease that causes shortness of breath and long-term breathing problems. She would still be there to take them golfing, but only with a cart. And she was still there on the sideline at any sporting event, with her oxygen machine, cheering on her grandkids.

One weekend, we had gone to see Joe at prep school, up in Maine, about three hours away. On our drive home, I received a call from my brother that my mom had not been able to catch her breath and had been admitted to the hospital. I was so mad that he had not called me earlier, but she had told him not to, because she did not want us to cut our trip short. Which she knew I would have done. Of course, I immediately called and went to see her as soon as we got home. She'd had an episode where she could not catch her breath, and she was put on a machine for a day or so to help her breathe.

On one of these visits to see my mom, Garret, who was around seven at the time, came with me. He wanted to get her a gift, so we looked around and I had to keep reminding him that it was a gift for Grammy, not for him. Eventually, he found a little square wooden sign that said, "Love you to the beach and back." This was one of her favorite sayings. And also, her favorite place in the world to go. She loved the beach. Mom grew up in New Jersey and had summered in Woods Hole down the Cape. We had moved to Massachusetts when I was seven and had lived in the coastal New England town we now called home. So we both knew she would love this sign. Garret also found a love stone. It was a silver, flat stone with the word *love* engraved on it. It would help her relax and remember to breathe if she got overwhelmed. It was a wishing stone, or what some people call a worry rock, but I reminded her to think about what she did want and not what she didn't. We came back up from the gift shop, and she opened her presents. She was so happy. She loved them, especially because G had picked them out for her all by himself.

Mom got better, but they wanted her to go to a rehab facility for a while to do some physical therapy and get better. I would go every night to see her. My boys would take turns coming with me. My brother and his kids would go, and she would light up every time one of her grandkids came in to see her. We would stay and chat and bring her much better food than they were offering. Mom always had her "Love you to the beach and back" sign next to her bed, and her love stone was always close by when she wasn't rubbing it.

When she got to go back home, she kept both on the nightstand next to her bed. She also needed some help showering and taking care of her apartment, so we would go over often and help her. I would go alone sometimes, and we would get to have some girl time. We had not gotten to do that in a long time. We used to get appetizers and a drink at the bar and catch up. I remember the last time we did that; it was always so much fun. But now she really couldn't do that anymore. It was hard to see this woman, who had always been so active, be restricted. However, over the next couple of months, she bounced back. And she even drove herself to Connecticut to see some friends and spend the weekend.

That was what made it so difficult to fathom when she passed away a week later. We had spent the Fourth of July together at my brother's house with all her grandkids. Afterward, over the next few days, I could not get hold of her. I thought my brother was going to go over, and he thought I was, and the next thing we knew, it had been three or four days, and no one had heard from her, which was so not like her. I had a feeling something was wrong, but she had lived on her own for years, and I'd had this feeling many times, and had driven over, only to find her sitting on her couch and playing sudoku. So I brushed the feeling off, figuring she was just busy with a doctor's appointment or going to lunch with a friend. Plus, she had gotten aggravated with all of us at the cookout, so I figured she just wanted some space to cool off.

When she had still not returned my or my nephew's calls and was about to miss another one of Joe's baseball games, I had to go check on her. I had my youngest son and my youngest nephew with me for the afternoon. I told myself that if I had not heard back from her by the afternoon, I'd swing over on my way after taking Brady to his mom's. I still had Garret with me. I think I figured, in some strange way, that if I had him with me, she would have to be OK. Once I got there and there was no answer, I started to panic. I asked the neighbor if she had seen my mom, and she said she had not seen her in a couple of days. My heart sank even more. I asked her to watch Garret for a minute while I went in through the bathroom window.

I found my mom in her apartment. She had passed away. It was the most horrible thing ever. My nephew had also been concerned and had said to call him once I got there. I phoned the police in hysterics, and then I had to call my nephew, my brother, and my husband. Joe was playing baseball, and when he saw his dad just up and leave, he knew something was very wrong. My nephew, my mom's oldest grandchild, came to the apartment first with his mom, and then my brother and my husband, and Joe. I had Joe get his little brother at the neighbor's house and go for a ride. I did not want them to see that. Years before, I had seen my grandmother after she had passed away in the hospital, and I just feel like a child should remember their life, not their death.

My oldest nephew was an adult. It was his choice, but I still wish he had not seen her like that. Even as an adult, it is an extremely difficult situation, to say the least. I was mad at her for not being happy the last time she had been with us. I was mad at her for being stubborn and using the spray paint with the wrong mask with her COPD, which most likely lead to her having a lack of oxygen and a heart attack. I was mad that I didn't get to say goodbye. Or possibly, that she didn't have to say goodbye just yet. I was mad at myself for not listening to my instincts. I was mad at everything. What if I had gone sooner? What if we had tried harder to make her listen when we had said spray-painting was not a good idea? She had always been fiercely independent, but she had gotten crazier over the past few years. She was always stubborn, but she seemed irrational at times.

A friend, who also had a mom with COPD, explained to me that the lack of oxygen to the brain actually does affect the person and make them sometimes say or do things that seem irrational or not like themselves. It made sense to me. Before her words, I had just not realized that this had been from the disease. I just thought it had been her getting older. How I wish I had understood her illness more. How I wish I could go back and change a few things. How I wish I could hear her voice and feel her soft hair on my cheek as she kissed me hello or goodbye. How I wish I could hear her laugh and see her crooked-toothed, beautiful smile one more time.

A few years earlier, I had been watching Wayne Dyer. He told a story about a woman he had been introduced to, and who had an amazing near-death experience. Her name was Anita Moorjani, and she had written a book called *Dying To Be Me*. I had given it to my mom, and she had read it, too. In

101

her book, Anita explains how the spirit goes on and never dies. She tells how the death experience was not frightening to experience, but if anything, it was liberating and a wonderful experience. I also learned this from listening to Abraham Hicks, another spiritual, personal development teacher I love.

They always say that death is just a transition from the physical form to the spirit form. We are actually more spiritual here in our bodies than we are physical. We are both spiritual and physical beings here on this earth, but always more spiritual and forever spiritual. Our spirit lives on long after this body, and long after this physical life. Our spiritual body lives forever. I have heard of people getting signs from loved ones who have transitioned or passed on. My friend Lisa saw hummingbirds at the craziest times after her mom passed on. I had also given her the book, *Dying To Be Me.* She loved the book because it showed her a perspective she had never considered before. It opened her mind up to what it means that our spirit lives forever. That we are all one, and intricately tied to all that is.

Garret was amazing during this time. He tried to lift everyone up and comfort them. He was always seeing if everyone was OK, and he was the youngest. My nephew saw a figure of an old woman come sit on a stool at the end of his bed in his room the morning she passed. It wasn't until later that day that he found out she had passed. In hindsight, he felt it had been her. As he was the oldest and had the biggest connection with her, it made so much sense to me that she would go see him in spirit form. I think this would have frightened any of the other kids, but not Bren. He had seen a spirit before, and she knew that. We had a celebration of life for my mom at the funeral home, and we showed a video I had put together. There were also collages and pictures of her life that the kids had made. We had a beautiful picture of her for everyone to remember her in life and not in her death. It was the hardest day of my life. My brother and I each wrote letters to my mom and read them out loud at her service.

This is what I wrote and read through my tears; this is what I wish I could have said to my mom in life but knew she would still hear in spirit:

> I'm feeling very blessed. The outpouring of loving memories, kind words, and love from friends, old friends, old neighbors, family we haven't seen in a long while, dear friends, people I've never met but knew my mom, so many

people that my mom's life touched, my brother and I can't say thank you enough! Every single note, whether to me or my cousins or a text to my brother, every phone call, it all means so much to all of us! My mom was a kindhearted, loving person! She loved to help people, taking in strays; you know who you are, lol! And loving them like her own! I remember being a teenager, and her reaching out to help my friend, and feeling at first like, *Hey I'm your daughter, not her,* almost a jealous-type feeling, but knowing that my friend needed help. I learned that her loving other people never took away her love from me, and it just added to it!

She wore her heart on her sleeve! Yes, she could be stubborn and fiercely passionate, that's why I never discussed politics with her, but that's also what made her who she was and love so very deeply and feel her emotions so deeply. If she didn't love so much, she couldn't have felt so hurt at times either! Well, I'd rather feel real hurt and know I have loved so deeply than to not feel anything! I know I loved her so much because otherwise I couldn't hurt so much right now! I never thought this day would come like it did. The positive is she didn't suffer. She was in her home. She left a legacy of love and kindness. She would talk about people we had never met like we were supposed to know who the hell they were. She did this because she did love everyone like they were her family! She made friends easily and quickly! She had a beautiful smile and a funny, quick wit and a loving zest for life! She was passionate about life and lived it well!

She had strong beliefs, like when my brother Bill was little, and she took him to see the yo-yo guy. Yes, Bill was into yo-yoing! The guy just opened the yo-yo packages and dropped them in the parking lot. My mom was like, what the hell is wrong with that guy? You don't just litter. And she made the guy pick it up, and of course he did, because you don't mess with Karen!

When you needed a champion, she would be there for you, she would back you 100 percent! And she was a great person to have on your side; like I said, you don't mess with Karen! She was intelligent and funny; very quick-witted, so much so that sometimes people didn't catch on! Like at the recent stay in the rehab, she said to the nurse, "I resemble that remark." And the nurse, who was clearly used to dealing with less witty people, said, "You resent or resemble?" And Karen's like rolling her eyes, and thinking, *Yeah honey, like I don't know the English language!* She takes a breath and says, "No, honey, 'resemble.'" It was something about being old, and then you could see the girl's light bulb go off, and she finally caught on that Karen was being funny.

She was my mom, she comforted me, she cried with me, she held my hand, she held my babies' fat little hands, she took care of me, she drove me crazy, she made me mad, she made me smile, she laughed with me, she told me I was beautiful, she played with me, she coached me, she was happy for me or sad with me, she was always there for me, she was my friend, and I will carry her love for me in my heart forever! Thank you, Mom. Love you to the beach and back, forever!

I still can't read this without tears streaming down my face. I miss her every single day. I have tried to comfort my children in their grief—especially Garret, since, being the youngest, I feel it was hardest on him. After everyone had left the service that day, he asked to go up to the altar where we had her picture and a few of her favorite touch stones in remembrance of her.

He asked, "Mom, will you come with me?"

And I said, "Of course, honey."

And his little body and mind could not keep it together any longer. He finally broke down, sobbing and crying.

And I was like, *Oh, there it is!* I knew it had been coming. I knew he could not be that stoic for that long, especially not at eight years old.

Our cousins and closest friends helped us pack up her pictures and flowers to bring them over to the restaurant where we were gathering with everyone afterward. The kids were hopping into relative's cars, and as we were backing out of the parking space, someone said, "Where's Garret?" Holy crap, we just left him in the funeral parlor!

"Oh, my God!" I said to Colby. "Quick, run in there. Someone said he went to the bathroom. Stand outside and say you were waiting for him. Quick, before he notices."

Colby got there just in time, as Garret was coming out of the bathroom. He never knew we almost left him at the funeral parlor. I know my mom was laughing at this one. So typical of being the third child and youngest of them all. It made us all laugh at the end of the worst day of our lives. We needed that laugh, and I also think that was a way of my mom getting us to remember that, even in the most difficult of situations, there is always something to laugh at! I could almost hear her laughing right along with us.

For a long time, Garret kept her love stone with him in his room. I put up her "Love you to the beach and back" sign in my kitchen so I could see it every day. Slowly, he grew less transfixed on the stone, and he would put it in a drawer or in a little container, and I was afraid he would misplace it or lose it, so I eventually kept it with me. I put it in my purse with my hope stone, in a little pocket where I always knew where they were. I always had them both with me, love and hope.

One day, I found out a friend had been diagnosed with breast cancer. A few of us, all friends because our boys played soccer together, decided to take her out for lunch before her treatments started. We were having a nice lunch and gave her a gift basket that all the soccer families had pitched in on. There were great things in there, like aromatherapy and a weighted blanket. The conversation came around to how it is now being noted that a person's outlook or attitude has a huge impact on their outcome and recovery. Someone brought up something about wishing stones and how you can focus on them, and they can help keep your mind focused on the positives. I was like, "Oh, my gosh, I have two stones that I keep with me all the time." I told them the story of my hope stone, and how that was a huge wink from Spirit, and then I explained about my mom's love stone, and how it had helped her stay strong in her weakest moments. This friend knew my mom and understood what I was saying about how I felt her strength and resolve and determination in that stone when I rubbed it. I had an overwhelming feeling that I should give these stones to my friend. The thought just came to me, or came over me. Then I thought, *No, I can't do that. I have had them forever; they are like a part of me.* And then I had another thought: *That's exactly why you should give them to her. She needs them now, and you don't need them anymore.*

I had already reached in my bag and had them out to show the ladies. Then I placed them in her hands and said that she needed them now, and I wanted her to have them. The hope and love I had gotten from them over the years I was now passing on to her. She said no, she couldn't take them, but I was insistent. Love and hope are meant to be given away. That is how they grow. I knew my mom would be happy I had decided to give them to my friend. I only occasionally thought about not having them, and every time I would get a pang of regret, I'd get an even bigger sensation that I had done the right thing, and that passing them on felt so much better than holding on to them. I also told my friend that if it made her feel any better, she could give them back to me someday when she was done with them. But for now, hope and love were my gifts to her!

## CHAPTER 13

# A Mother's Love Is Forever!

. . . . . . . . . .

I thought giving away my mom's love stone might come back to bite me. What if Garret asked about it? If he did, I would just tell him that I felt my friend, who he also knows, needed it right now. I thought he would understand. He has not asked about it once. We have many other touch stones of our own to remember my mom by. Some are our things that we already had, and some are her things that we now have. At first, it was hard, but now it brings comfort to have something of hers, like an old sweatshirt or a coffee mug or a Christmas decoration, that brings back happy memories. I feel that a person leaves a part of them in everything they touch; they leave their energy in the object. When I wear one of my mom's sweatshirts, I feel like I am getting a nice, big, warm hug from her.

Soon after she passed, I had some dreams. They were so real. I saw her and felt her, like it was happening in the physical world, and then I would wake up. But it was not like any dream I had ever had before. It was not like déjà vu. It was like I felt her hugging me. She had on something red, and I could smell her vanilla perfume. Then I awoke, and I was no longer with her. I was in my bed. But I had felt her, as real as anything I have ever felt in the physical world. It was amazing, and I found myself looking forward to going to sleep to have these encounters. I still have very vivid dreams of my mom, but none as realistic as those I'd had shortly after her passing. It was like she was coming to comfort me. She was coming to tell me everything was all right, that she was not mad at me, and although she did not mean for this to happen, it was her time.

I always felt like somehow, if I had been there, this would not have happened. She reassured me it was not my fault and that nothing anyone could have done would have changed the outcome. Even if I had been with her in the moment it happened, I could not have prevented the outcome. I always knew she had been afraid of death, and she did not want to die alone. I think that was—and is—the hardest thing for me. Not necessarily that she is gone, even though obviously that is hard, but that I was not there with her when she left. I wondered if she was scared in those last moments. Did she know what was happening? I just wish I could have been with her. She was with me for my first breath, and for the first breath of my last baby. I wish I could have been there for her when she took her last breath to comfort her, as she now comforts me in my dreams. I know my mom lives on through me and my brother and our children. I see her mannerisms in the mirror and hear her voice come out of my mouth much too often. I heard this even before she passed. I will never forget the day I said something that sounded just like my mother. "Because I said so!" It came flying out of my mouth before I could help myself, and I then gasped and covered my mouth and rolled my eyes at myself (if that's even possible). And I have said and done many things that give away my lineage if you knew my mom.

One time, after she passed, I was cleaning up and going through some of her things that had ended up in my brother's garage when I came across a letter she had written to his second wife before they got married. It talked about him as a little kid in his Batman costume, and other little cute things about him as a child. I had never known she had written the letter, and it was awesome. I then thought I would like to find something like this about me, so I know she felt I was a good daughter. Like I had said earlier, we had some rough patches in our lives, and I just wanted to know that she knew I loved her and that none of that other stuff mattered. All that mattered was her love. Well, soon after, I found a book that she had given me and had tucked away in a drawer. The title was *The Love between a Mother and Daughter Is Forever.* On the inside cover is a poem.

The relationship between
a mother and daughter
is comprised of a very deep
understanding of and support for
each other
It is based on an enormous
amount of emotion and love
There is no other relationship
in the world
where two women are so much
like one
—Susan Polis Schutz

She had written my name at the top and put parentheses around this poem, and then she had written underneath it:

I think this says it all!! But every page of this book expresses
& says it all too. Enjoy
Love, Mom

I remember saying out loud, "Thanks, *Mom*!" I had asked for something, and then I found this book. Again, I felt this was Spirit sending me a message, but this time it was my mom's spirit coming through.

Another amazing thing that happened after my mom passed came from my niece Alison when she went to see a psychic. Ali was in her early twenties at the time, recently graduated from college, and she just wanted some clarification on the direction she should go in life. At the time, we both worked for her family's restaurant. It was a few days after her session with the psychic. She had told me at the beginning of the shift that she wanted to tell me something from her reading.

Ali knew my mom well. Like I have explained, she loved all her grandkids, even the ones who were not technically hers. She loved my nieces on my husband's side like they were her own, too.

I could not wait. I said to her, "No, tell me now!"

She asked, "OK? Are you sure?"

"Yes, please!" I said.

It was fairly quiet at the time, and I was anxious to hear. So she told me a few things the psychic had told her about her career path and what city she was going to take a job in, fun things, but it was also crazy how the psychic knew things. See, Ali had gone to college in South Carolina, and she had made connections in that area, and we are in New England. So this psychic seemed like she was right on with those things.

She told me a few other things I forget now, and then she said, "She told me something about Gramma Karen."

Of course, at this I started crying.

Ali said, "I didn't want to make you cry."

I said, "Ali, you know I'm a crier, anyway. I'm gonna cry, no matter what you tell me."

She smiled and said, "She told me Karen is with all the babies. She said not to worry, she is taking care of all the babies."

Now, streams of tears were just leaking from my face as I gasped. *How the hell could Ali know that?*

I do not even think Ali understood the extent to which I'd had miscarriages. Ali is the same age as my oldest son Joe, so she knew I had fertility issues and had miscarried. But for her to say babies—plural—was even crazier! There was nothing my mom loved more than her grandchildren, and this was confirmation that, no matter where her soul was, she was happy! I do not think Ali knew the significance of what she told me. Still, she definitely knew it had hit home.

She looked at me when I had that amazed look of shock on my face, like how the heck could this person have known that, and she said, "I know, right!"

She knew this was a message from Karen, too. It sent shivers down my spine and still gives me goose bumps and tears to this day. It was an unexpected supernatural experience that I will forever be grateful for. Love does go on forever. Love knows no bounds. It does not end. Even with death, it lives on. I can still feel my mother's love in my heart, even though she has left this physical world and has transitioned to the nonphysical.

Another way I know she is still with me is all the signs I get. Shortly after her passing, I would constantly see the number forty-four, the year of her birth. I would also see sevens. She was seventy-two when she passed, in the month of July, in the year 2017. I would see these numbers when

I was thinking of her, not specifically asking for a sign, but just having a fond memory. I would think of something funny that had happened, or a song would come on the radio that would make me smile and think of her, and then I would see these signs. When I was scared or nervous, like when I had to have a biopsy because my OB thought I might have uterine fibroids, I went into the office, and the number on my file was 4747, or 4477, or some combination, and I knew it was a message from my mom that it was going to be OK. I did not ask to see the number, I just happened to glance over at one point and saw it. I then had a wave of calm come over me, and I knew everything was all right, that she was watching over me and looking out for me, still. The procedure showed I did have uterine fibroids, and it was recommended that I should have them removed, to stop my painful, heavy periods. The day of the procedure, I was completely calm and worry-free. I had learned to listen to my inner voice, and my mom was speaking to me loudly and clearly from beyond that it was all going to be OK, that it was all good!

Signs were everywhere over the years. My son Colby had his first high school varsity soccer game that year, the first game my mom was not there for. I know I was greatly aware of missing her presence at this game. It was a beautiful, sunny day with big, wispy clouds and a bright blue sky. At the game, I happened to look up at the sky, thinking how crazy it was that she was not there to see him play. When I glanced up, the clouds were so wispy, like nothing I had ever seen, and then I noticed they were in the shape of an angel. She was watching! I took a picture, and you can see the head and face, and these massive wings along both sides of her body, as she's looking down. It was another moment of awe and wonder at the way Spirit was showing me life goes on beyond this physical realm.

Another sign came to me that following spring. Joe was down in Florida for his spring break baseball tournament. He was with his college team playing D2 baseball, a dream of his which she never got to see. He had also not hit a home run before in his life. We could only watch on Live Stats, not on a video. (Live Stats is like the Marauder's Map from *Harry Potter*, but in digital form. It shows an online outline of the baseball field with labels saying who is in what position, who is up to bat, and who is on each base.) Joe got up to bat and hit his first home run, ever!

He recounted the actual events to us later, and he told us that as he rounded the bases, he felt his grammy smiling down on him, and he impulsively tapped his chest and blew a kiss, pointing up to the sky in honor and remembrance of her. It was a beautiful moment. I know he felt her presence with him, just like I did when I saw that amazing angel cloud in the sky. The signs will be different for everyone, but trust that when a loved one transitions from this physical plane, they will send messages or signs to you. It will be something meaningful to you, so you will know beyond a shadow of a doubt that it is a message from your loved one from somewhere beyond this place and time, from the place we all come from and the place we shall one day return to.

My mom's favorite place was the beach. I now live up the hill from the beach she loved the most, Humarock. We had lived there together after my parent's divorce, and she had also lived there in other rental properties over the years. It was her happy place. After her passing, I would go for long walks down to the beach, look out at the horizon, and think of her. I would often go by myself, but we also loved going on family walks there as well. When my cousins would come visit, no matter what time of year it was, we would go for a walk there. In fact, the last time my mom saw my cousin Steph (and her daughter, son-in-law, and baby Levi) was at Humarock. They had come for a visit in the spring. It was warm for New England; it was sweatshirt weather. My mom loved Levi! He was her only sister's great-grandson, which made her a great-aunt. Did I tell you how much my mom loves the babies? She was in her glory, even though, because of her oxygen tank, she could not come all the way down. She still loved getting to see them from the seawall. Levi and my boys, who absolutely adore him, were playing in the surf. It was warm enough to feel the water, and Levi got caught by a wave and unexpectedly got his sneakers wet. He did not care, he wanted to take off all his clothes and go in. It was still a little too chilly for that, but he had a great time, anyway. When we left that day, Mom held one of Levi's fat, little hands, and my cousin's daughter Sara (his mom) held his other fat, little hand as we walked back home.

We have so many fond memories there, it seems fitting that this was the last place they had spent time together. I took a picture of them walking home hand in hand with little Levi, the next generation in the middle, and it now means so much to me.

112

I started going for walks to clear my head, and I would feel closer to my mom at the beach. On one of these walks, I was thinking about her, and it was after I had given the hope and love stones to my friend. I was thinking about that and wondering how my mom would feel about it. I know I said I thought she would be fine with it, but it was also the stone Garret had given her. Should I have kept it for him? I thought then, when my friend gets better, she will give it back to us, and someday she still might. I guess I was having some mixed emotions about it and wondering if, from his perspective, he'd be upset about it—and I would completely understand that. But I also thought this could be a life lesson about helping others, too. Anyway, all those thoughts were going through my mind as I was walking along, and I looked down to see a heart-shaped rock staring up at me.

Humarock is aptly named because there are so many damn rocks, and right there in front of me was a heart-shaped rock. I know people find them, but I do not think it is that common. (Or maybe it is?) However, I was questioning things in my head, and it was like my mom's spirit said, *Here, stop worrying.* She gave me a heart stone. It was so fitting. I know ... crazier things have happened, right? LOL! What makes this even more amazing is that I literally cannot go to the beach without finding a heart-shaped rock. Every single time I go, I find one or more. I have an entire collection of heart-shaped rocks, from teeny-tiny ones to ones the size of my fist. Sometimes, I look down, with a knowing that I will see one.

It got to a point, though, that I was looking down at my feet and missing the beautiful horizon and birds, the sand and the clouds, and the different shades of blue in the ocean with the waves crashing. I had a block of thought that suggested I should stop looking at my feet all the time and enjoy the sights and sounds, especially when my family was with me, to enjoy the people I was with. I still find a heart-shaped rock every time I go to the beach, and it does not just happen at Humarock. I find heart-shaped rocks at every beach I go to, whether in my hometown, or on Nantucket, or anywhere! This was—and still is—a message from my mother that it was completely fine to give my special hope and love rocks to my friend, and that she has given me something else instead, something even more special.

I know they are just rocks, but to me they are so much more. They are this amazing sign that a mother's love never dies. It gives me a sense of comfort about life that I cannot truly explain in words. I also see heart shapes everywhere, not just in rocks. One day, I was cleaning out the soot from the fireplace, and there was a chunk of black, cindered wood that was in the shape of a heart. I keep it on my mantle. Other times, I have found heart-shaped pieces of lettuce in a salad. I have found a heart-shaped rock buried in the grass. There have been paint splatters on the ground in the shapes of hearts. I even have a heart-shaped freckle on my shoulder that I only noticed after I got my flu shot, because who is ever looking at the outside of their shoulder? Crumbs from a sandwich, rays from the sun, shadows, spatters of sauce, anything and everything. I am always looking, not trying to make it happen, but being open-minded about it happening. And every time I see a heart shape, I know it is a sign from my mom.

Of course, my children think I am crazy, and I will admit, with some rocks you have to use your imagination a little more, but to me, they are all signs, whether they are perfectly symmetrical or a little lopsided. Whether they are rocks or ashes or lettuce, I could not make them happen if I tried. I just have an open mind about seeing them. And every time I do, I get a little smile across my face, and I think of my mom, if I had not been already. This is her way of sending signs to me personally, and I know it. Whether anyone else ever believes it or not, I do not care. I will usually nudge my husband or point it out to him and say, "Hey, Paul, do you see that?" And he sees them, too, and he smiles with me, and we remember my mom and all the love she has for all of us, and we feel comforted by the knowing that her love never dies.

Love never dies. Just close your eyes and think of someone you love or have loved, or just think of love, and you can feel your heart swell up and your lungs fill with gratitude, and you will know what a blessing and a gift this life truly is. I now know that the love I have felt between a mother and a child—whether I was the mother or the child, whether that child came into physical being or not, whether the mother is still here in physical form or not—transcends all things, lasts forever, and is what life is all about!

"Your Mother Is Always with You"
Deborah R. Culver

She's the whisper of the leaves as
you walk down the street.
She's the smell of certain foods
you remember, flowers, you pick,
the fragrance of life itself.
She's the cool hand on your brow when
you're not feeling well.
She's your breath in the air on a cold
winter's day.
She is the sound of the rain that lulls you
to sleep, the colors of a rainbow.
She is Christmas morning.
Your mother lives inside your laughter.
She's the place you come from,
your first home.
She's the map you follow with every
step you take.
She's your first love, your first friend,
even your first enemy.
But nothing on Earth can separate you.
No time.
No space.
Not Even death.

## CHAPTER 14

# A Blessing or a Curse, It's Up to You!

· · · · · · · · ·

When I was around five or six years old, my brother and I had to have surgery on our ears. We were both born with what they called a "shell" ear. We lacked cartilage in the upper, outer part of the ear. The surgeon pinned back our ears and formed the cartilage so we would have more "normal" looking ears that would not be so prominent. When we went to visit the hospital to see what would happen when we had our actual appointment, I saw something that frightened me. A male nurse was yelling at a kid for climbing out of her hospital crib-bed, and he was very stern. When this happened, it was like I got tunnel vision, and my eyesight zoomed in on him yelling at her. I remember distinctly thinking that I hoped that would not happen to me. Well, of course, the time came for us to have our surgeries, and my brother and I shared a recovery room.

I do not know how my mom did it. It was the 1970s, and at that time, parents did not stay in the hospital with their kids. My mom had to leave both of us in the hospital room overnight, without her. When we came out of surgery, we had to drink about five Dixie cups full of juice, and then they would take the IV out. I sucked mine down, no problem. But my brother started coughing and choking on the second or third cup, so he had to leave his IV in. During the night, he woke up and said he had to go to the bathroom. He could not go himself, as he was still hooked up to his IV. So, being the good sister that I am, I climbed over the rail and out of my bed to get someone to help him. As soon as I walked out of the doorway to our room, I ran into that same male nurse, and he yelled at me, word for word, how he had yelled at the little girl on the day we had visited.

It was like déjà vu. It was the first time I had ever experienced this. It felt weird, like I somehow knew it was going to happen, or possibly that I had made it happen, as if my focusing on it happening to someone else, even though I did not want it to happen to me, had unknowingly attracted it. Whatever way you look at it, there was a connection between me seeing this happen earlier and the same thing then happening to me. It felt like a supernatural, physic type of knowing. When it was happening to me, I knew exactly what he was going to say, and I just sat there with an open-mouthed look of shock and surprise on my face, and I could not believe it was happening. The male nurse just thought I was taken aback because he had caught me out of bed, but it was much more than that.

When I was seven, I had warts all over the heel of one foot and on the arch of the other. My mom had taken me to a doctor who was not a pediatrician. He was either a dermatologist (skin doctor) or a podiatrist (foot doctor), but he definitely was not a pediatrician (kid's doctor). He had put me up on a moving table and tried to burn or freeze the warts off, but when I turned my head around and saw the blood, I screamed and tried to jump off the table that was now many feet in the air. He then yelled at me to sit still, and I started crying. He stopped and put the table down. We all knew this was not going to work.

Then, one night, my parents happened to watch *The Tonight Show Starring Johnny Carson*. His guest was recounting a story about a friend whose kid had warts all over his arm. To get rid of the warts, he drew a picture of his arm with the warts, and then he put the picture in the fire and said a prayer of thanks for them going away. In a few weeks, the warts were gone. This made my mom do some research about these types of things. She came across a method she thought would work for me. On the night of a full moon, I was to take a raw potato and cut it in half, rub it ten times to the right and ten times to the left on each wart, then bury the potato outside under a tree, and the warts would go away.

So, on the night of the next full moon, I did this. I genuinely believed this would make my warts go away, and they did! I was now wart-free, and although I did not realize it at the time, I had just had my first experience with the immense power of mind over matter! I had just controlled my

117

outer world with my inner thoughts. My parents did not even know exactly why this had worked. They were simply happy because I had been so picky with my feet, and they now thought I would be less particular because my feet would not hurt so much. Whenever I would later tell someone this story, they would ask how, or why, it had happened, and some would even suggest it had something to do with the starch in the potato. I even thought, *Well, maybe. But if this was actually the case, then why has someone not bottled potato juice as a wart remover and made a million bucks?*

When I took Joe for his one-year checkup, I had the déjà vu, tunnel vision experience again. This was the time when I saw the other mom with her young child, and the doctor saying she had a very sick child and would have to get him to the hospital right away. Then, about two weeks later, the same thing happened to us. Once again, it was word for word what I had heard said to someone else, and I had thought, *God, I hope that never happens to me!* But it did happen, exactly word for word, like I somehow knew this, or I had been given an insight from Spirit. Each time this happened, I only recalled it happening once it was happening to me. I would think, *I have heard this before*, and I would have a vision of seeing and hearing it the first time, when I had been strictly an observer. Now I was a participant in the same exchange, and I was having the same experience I had observed.

The next time I had something like this happen was when I was in the hospital with Joe when he was sick, and I had the thoughts about the person who was a friend of a friend who'd had an issue with her liver. As it turned out, Joe had liver failure, and I somehow knew this before it was possible for me to know it. The doctors did not know yet; they had not done tests yet, so it was impossible to know this information when I knew it. But within that word *impossible* are the words *I'm possible*. And, from my life experiences, I know now that anything is possible!

Why did I have all these experiences? What was the reason? What was the purpose? Did I focus on what I did not want out of overwhelming fear, and inadvertently attracted those same situations to me? Was it more basic than that? Was it just that I was on the same vibration, or energy, level? Or maybe I had these experiences so I would have an open mind about these types of things happening, so I would learn how to tune into my inner voice, or spirit, when I heard it. There is definitely room for interpretation. But it is my interpretation, and how I feel about it is what matters most for me. Someone else can tell me what they think, or why they think these events happened, but they are not me. Only I can know what I was thinking and how I was feeling at the time I had these visions or hypersensitive, sensational experiences. From when I was a child to when I was an adult, I would have these times when I somehow knew before the knowing would be possible in the physical world, and I feel they were somehow messages from Spirit. They only seemed to happen when I was in some type of emergency or crisis, some extreme life-or-death situation.

Even when I thought I was not listening to my gut, like when my mom passed away, I think there was a reason. At the time of her death, both my middle son and my niece (who are the same age) were going to sports camps. I often thought I should have felt her leaving this world, or I would have gotten some type of a message from Spirit right when this happened, but I did not. It was a couple of days later, and I doubted those impulses that were telling me something was wrong. If we had found out earlier, the kids would not have gone to their sports camps, and you know how much she loved them playing their sports. I believe that she did not want us to know until later because, even in death, she did not want to have them miss their camps. I know this may sound trivial to some or most, but if you knew her, you would understand, whether you would agree with me or not.

My brother and I both had to pick up our fifteen-year-old kids from camp and tell them that their grandma had passed away. It was one of the hardest things either of us had ever had to do, but we both agreed not to pick them up early because she would not have wanted us to do that. We were upset that she had been mad at all of us because the kids would not pose for a picture on the Fourth of July, the last time she saw any of us. I actually said out loud to my husband that day, "I can't believe she is being this mad. What if this is the last time she sees any of us?"

She had just yelled bye and waved from the deck where she had been having a conversation with Joe and Brennan. That was unlike her. She would always give lots of hugs and kisses goodbye. Now, in hindsight, it was such a synchronistic moment, and one I know I will never forget. Because we knew she was upset with all of us, but mostly the kids, we knew it would not last. She could never stay mad at them. They knew she could be cranky sometimes. Now I know it was most likely due to her disease rather than her personality. I only wish I had understood that at the time.

When I had called my nephew, asking about the last time he had spoken to her, he agreed with me that she was probably still a little aggravated with all of us, and that was why she wasn't answering our texts. Plus, she had tried to get my brother, my nephew, me, and Joe to help her with a project which we all agreed she should not be doing. She was trying to repurpose an old microwave cart that was literally falling apart. She loved doing these types of projects, but we all felt it was not a good idea. She had tried to get us to come over and help her move it, but it had to be on that day because it was outside, and the guys were coming to do the lawn, and it could not be in their way. Since we all could not get there, we figured she was a little annoyed with us for this also. I thought my brother or nephew had gone to help her because I knew Joe and I both could not fit it in that day.

It was not until later that I realized none of us had gone. Then, when she was ignoring not only my phone calls but also my nephew's calls, I really started to worry that something was wrong, and that she was not just ticked off. If any one of these details were off slightly, could it have changed the outcome? Unfortunately, we will never know. But what we do know is that my mom had always said she did not want to be one of those cranky old people who slowly loses touch with reality. She did not want to lose her mind to old age. I think she transitioned before this happened to her because that was how she had wanted it. I do not think she wanted to die, or leave when she did, but I believe she went out on her terms. She had been doing what she loved up until the end, traveling and visiting friends just the weekend before and refurbishing old furniture. And then, just like that, she transitioned. She did not suffer or lose her mind. And when I explained the situation to my doctor, who had been the primary care doctor for each of us, she said that, even if someone had been there with her, it still would have happened. Even if an EMT had been there at the time, she still would have passed.

Was this a blessing, that she had gone quickly and had not suffered? She had lived a very full life, but none of us ever thought she would go when she did. None of us got to say goodbye. Is it better to know someone is dying, like when my aunt had ovarian cancer, and we had to watch her suffer and fade away into a former shadow of herself, but those left behind had some form of closure? Or is it better to just go unexpectedly? But then those left behind are left with so many questions. They are both hard experiences, and neither seems fair. It is not our job to know the reasons why, but it is our job to find the good!

Why does anything happen the way it does? Why did Joe get so sick as a baby? Why had we had such a rough road to parenthood? Why had I had those synchronistic experiences as a child, and again as an adult? I think I know the reason. I believe all these experiences happened for the good of it all. How can something so horrible possibly be good? You have to look for it. At the time, it was awful, every one of these circumstances was awful! No one can argue that. But what came from them was good. A connection to Spirit. An understanding that life is just a result of the energy level you are at, and if you want to change your life, you only need to look at it differently. It can be a blessing or a curse, it is up to you.

When I was a kid and had all those warts, at the time, it felt like a curse. But, in time, I was able to see it as a blessing because at a young age I was learning to tune into my inner spirit. I was learning how powerful my mind was, although I would not fully understand this until years later. When I had those tunnel vision, zoomed-in experiences, they were definite blessings because they gave me that sense of knowing before I could otherwise have known it. Although at the time they were pretty scary incidents, again, I was learning to tune into my inner voice.

At times throughout my life, I have ignored this inner voice and went against it, like when I gave myself all those fertility drugs when I had worked so hard at getting healthy. From those experiences, however, I have learned that going through with something when it does not feel good, when it causes inner conflict, is a sign to stop. A good outcome cannot come from a bad feeling. And when I had the tubal, it was definitely a horrible experience, one of the most gut-wrenching, heartbreaking situations of my life, but in the long run, I believe that, even if I had the cyst from birth, the fertility drugs caused that cyst to grow exponentially and become life-threatening. If not for the tubal, and all the synchronicities of that situation, I would not be here, so how can I see this as anything but a blessing now? I give thanks and appreciation for the blessing of this little soul every day!

Another time, when Joe was in high school, I had picked him up from school. Things were not going his way. He had not been put on the varsity baseball team as a junior. He was devastated. He was good and understood the game better than anyone I knew. He had been given the option to stay down on junior varsity and get reps down there, getting called up when needed. Or, the coach said he had a varsity jersey for him, but he would not be a starter, he would have to sit. Joe decided he would sit on varsity and be there for the call. He looked at me and said, "I figured, what the heck, Mom. I'm not supposed to be here, anyway, so I might as well go for it. I've got nothing to lose."

He knew he had almost died as an infant. I looked him in the eyes and said, "Oh no, Joe! You are most certainly supposed to be here, or you would not be. And yes, you should follow your gut and go for it!"

I know it sounds like semantics, but it is more than that; it is perspective. Whether you think you are not supposed to be here because you had a near-death experience but survived, or if you think you are most certainly supposed to be here because you survived after a near-death experience, your perspective makes all the difference in the world. The first way of looking at it is negative, and the second is positive. A positive perspective or outlook on life changes your life! Joe took this originally disappointing situation and made the best of it. He lived. He did not almost die; he lived! And there is a difference between these perspectives. He found the good, and he played varsity.

You would think the diagnosis of an extremely rare metabolic disorder would be a curse. Especially since I have explained all the numbers involved. Not only did we meet and have babies, but we also now know all three of our boys have the metabolic disorder! All three! The chance of Paul and I meeting and both having the same bad recessive gene is one in a million. Each of our children's possibility of getting the disorder was only 25 percent for each child, yet all three of them have it. I cannot even think about the numbers. Normal math makes me nauseous as it is. The odds are astronomical that this would happen. So this tells me that odds do not matter, especially when you are that one in a million, or more!

Our metabolic doctor has told us that if our boys have what he suspects their disorder is, they would be in a very exclusive club of about ten to twelve people in the entire world. Only about eight or nine other people have the same disorder. We do not know, and perhaps we will never know, because of lack of testing. There is a genome study that we have participated in, but it showed nothing the last time we checked. They will rerun or cross-reference Joe's sample as he is the one who had the initial illness, and Colby and Garret can only have what he has. If it does not show up on Joe's blood work, it would not be in theirs. Every day there are new tests identifying more and more, and hopefully we will get answers in our lifetime; but if not, then maybe it will help someone else in the future. As for now, my boys are healthy and happy, and we know how to manage their disorder. On the positive side, it also has helped with the drinking and drug issues that kids can get into in their teens. As my boys know, they cannot put their bodies in a situation that would cause them to vomit, so they have never wanted to be big partiers. It has helped us stay on top of our health, nutrition, and physical fitness. And when one of my kids would ask about how an alcoholic beverage tastes, we would let them try it, at home. We have an extremely open and honest relationship with our boys. We support each other, and we respect each other's opinions and (as two of them are legal adults) their choices.

In the long run, the metabolic disorder has brought us together and forced us to find the humor in some crazy situations. It has put us on a path that we most likely would not have been on, but one that reminds us to live our best lives every day. For that, I am supremely thankful and appreciative. I remember thinking back to when I was an active member of the FOD support group, and I felt so utterly devastated and sad for every single family that was now going through what we had gone through. I made a decision at the time that I could not have my everyday life be about the worst thing that had ever happened to us. But what if the worst thing to happen was actually the best thing?

What if, because of all the shit, we learned to love and appreciate all the little things in life that we otherwise would have taken for granted? Like being happy and laughing together, and spending time with each other. Whether we are boating, fishing, playing cards, or just having dinner together, I am happiest when we are all together, and I know this will never change! So, for all of it, I am thankful. I can be thankful for the rain, because without it, I would never see the rainbow! So blessing or curse? It is all up to you and how you decide to look at whatever life circumstance you are living at the moment, and know it is always changing. Nothing lasts forever, so focus on the good, and find things that make you happy, because life is too much of a blessing to spend a second of it without a grateful and happy heart. For me, I choose to see it all as a blessing every single time!

---

CHAPTER 15

---

## *Extraordinary Possibilities*

• • • • • • • • • •

Once you realize that you can control your thoughts, and therefore, what vibrational energy you are giving out, this is how you control your life circumstances, and your life will change. I realized that I cannot change things that have happened, but I can change how I feel about them, and sometimes a little time and perspective is all that's needed to see more clearly.

Things can suck, things can most certainly be horrible, but I have realized that I do not have to stay in that place. I do not have to live there. I can acknowledge the shit, but once I know it is there, I do not have to keep stepping in it! I can walk around it or pick it up; I have choices. And my attitude allows me to be a vibrational match to the problem, the shit, or the solution—noticing the shit and stepping around it. If I focus on the shit, I will most likely step in it again, but if I focus on a nice, green lawn that is soft and well-manicured, with organic fertilizer, there will be no shit on my lawn. There is no room for shit in my beautiful image of my nice, organic, green lawn. Take focus off the unwanted and put it on what is wanted. I cannot think my kids' metabolic disorder away, but we can focus on all the positives that have come from it. Nothing will ever change the horror I had witnessed when my thirteen-month-old child almost died, but I can change the story to think about how amazing it is that he lived, and because of his ordeal he quite possibly saved his younger brothers from ever going through anything like that ever!

Why did certain things not work for me, and perhaps more importantly, why did the things work when they did? When I was using all those fertility drugs, I had an inner conflict. It did not feel good or right, but there was a part of me that felt it was better because there was possibly something wrong with my eggs. Even though I did not like putting those drugs in my body, I was also afraid to not follow the course the fertility doctors had outlined for me, because they were pulling out the best eggs and sperm and making the embryos that had the best chance of survival, or so I was being told.

When you have mixed emotions about something, you have no clarity. You feel conflicted and confused. When you are being told one thing, but you feel another, it causes confusion. I had such inner conflict that I believe this was why, even after the cyst was removed, I was unable to conceive. I did not feel good about it. Have you ever heard the saying, "Whether you think you can or you think you cannot, you are right"? Our beliefs have major influences on our life in physical form. If you believe you can or believe you cannot, the thought will affect your ability to do whatever it is your belief is about, so much more than we as a society realize at this moment in time. People, however, are beginning to realize this, and it is being documented more and more. Remember that doctor who told me to keep reading to Joe and playing him music and talking to him when he was sick, because it could be doing just as much good as the medicines, if not more? He understood this!

Life is what you believe it is! In every situation, in every person, there are things you like and things you do not like. It is our job to focus on the things that we like. It is our job to look for the wanted, and to look for the good, in all situations. This does not mean making yourself do something you do not like. Don't try to eat fried ants if you do not like the taste of them. Listen to your inner voice. Everyone is different. If you like guacamole, eat it, but don't try to tell everyone else how delicious it is if they do not like avocados. It is great that you like it, it's just not for everyone. That is the way it is supposed to be, and that is perfectly fine!

You can love ballet, and in sharing your love for ballet, those who also love it will learn from your enthusiasm and love of art. Those who do not will fall asleep during the performance. Not everything is for everyone. Everyone is unique in their own way. It is our job, as individuals, to tune into our own inner calling. It is our job, as parents, not to steer our children in the direction of what we want but in the direction of what they want. It is our job to guide them and get them to listen to their own inner voice. If you do not want to work but feel this is the only way you can make money, it is gonna be a tricky ride for you. But if you acknowledge money can come to you in a variety of ways, and a job is just one of them, and you then seek a job you will have fun at and love, then it will never feel like work. It will just be a fun way to make a living. Life is supposed to be fun!

In this vein, when I was trying so hard to conceive a child and had such conflict, it was never going to work for me. If I was totally OK with IVF drugs and had faith in all the science, then it probably would have worked for me. This is why many women are successful with IVF treatments all the time. But for me, it was like trying to make myself eat fried ants while knowing I do not like the taste of them.

When I finally had done all that I could do, and I had no choice but to let go and just love my life, that was when what I had wanted so badly came so easily to me without even trying. The key to having what you want is in the letting go of it. I know this sounds paradoxical, but when you are wanting and longing for something (in my case, to have another child), you are, in fact, acknowledging that you do not have it. But when you let go of the not having of it, you leave room for it to come to fruition in your reality. I let go of all my negative thinking that there was something wrong with me, and I focused on counting my blessings. In doing so, I allowed myself to be the mom I was and the mom I wanted to be.

I did not already have to be a mom to do this, but in my case, it did make it easier for me. When you use your imagination, the universe does not know if your feelings are coming from an imagined or a physical place. Your feelings are the language of your soul. Your emotions are the outcome of your feelings. Think about something right now that makes you laugh, whether from the past or in the future, and you will feel a smile spread across your face. You may even chuckle or laugh out loud, right here and now in the present moment. Think of something or someone that made you angry or sad, and you will feel those emotions right here and now.

Let go of the struggle! Let go of thinking it is going to be so hard. No matter what it is you are desiring, it will be. This does not mean it will fall into your lap; in this physical place, there is a space-time continuum that allows for a buffer of time. It can take minutes, hours, days, months, or years, however you feel about the desired outcome. There is also that thing called quantum physics, which is beyond the scope of this book. If you are interested in learning more on this subject, I suggest you look up anything from Dr. Joe Dispenza. Amazing!

In conclusion, I would like to say that, whatever your desired outcome is, it is possible. This is my favorite quote, and it is from Dr. John Eliot's book *Overachievement*:

"Overachievement is aimed at people who want to maximize their potential. And to do this I insist you throw caution to the wind, ignore the pleas of parents, coaches, spouses, and bosses to be 'realistic.' Realistic people do not accomplish extraordinary things because the odds of success stymie them. The best performers ignore the odds. I will show that instead of limiting themselves to what's probable, the best will pursue the heart-pounding, exciting, real big, difference-making dreams—so long as catching them might be possible!"

The definition of real is that which never changes. I argue that our physical reality is always changing, and therefore, it does not fit the definition. What is realistic is different for everyone, though we all come into this world the same. The only difference is what we believe is realistic for ourselves. What is real is our soul. If you were to lose a limb or have something that limits your physical body, you are still the same person inside. It may change your perspective or outlook on life, but you are the same inner spirit. You can acknowledge, by looking back at baby pictures, that your body has changed from birth to wherever you are in life right now, but you are still the same *you* inside. You can remember falling off that bike at six years old, or getting that hairline fracture in your ankle at seven, but you are not in that same body.

The things that happen to us physically shape how we feel about our experiences here in this world. But it does not have to define them. You can always have a greater expectation! Just because something happened once does not mean that is the way it has to be forever. Having one miscarriage does not mean you cannot have another baby. In fact, having multiple miscarriages, and multiple failed IUI treatments, and multiple failed IVF procedures only mean it did not work those times. It is not a condemnation for life. Just like your first painting is not an indication of your future artistic ability. We are only limited by our own imaginations of what we believe we are capable of accomplishing.

I believed that I could conceive another child. I stopped believing that there was something wrong with me. I started believing that what I wanted would come to me, and that I did not have to chase my dream, but the fact that I was having this dream meant it was possible for me. I did not have to go through all that, but that was what caused me to finally give myself permission to let go. Often, as human beings, we do not fully let go until we can say we have tried it all, or until we are backed into a corner. But we can create from inspiration or from motivation. Motivation is knowing that if you do not do something, something will go wrong; it is a pushing from outside of you. But inspiration is a pulling from within you. It can come from you or from someone else's story that speaks to your inner being, but it resonates with your calling from within. This was how I felt when I read Julia Indichova's book, *Inconceivable*. It felt like she had written it for me and was speaking directly to me. I could see myself in her, and I knew, if it was possible for her, then it was possible for me.

Anything is possible! I heard the great Wayne Dyer recount a story once about being interviewed. When Wayne said that anything was possible, the interviewer then said to him something along the lines of, "So, if I'm a five-foot four-inch, 150-pound, middle-aged man, I could play in the NFL?" And Wayne asked, "Is that believable to you?" Of course, the man said no. Wayne said, then it would not be. But the case in point is Spud Webb. Spud played in the NBA and is known for winning a slam dunk contest, despite being one of the shortest players to ever play, at five foot six inches tall. Was it likely that a man with a shorter stature would ever play in the NBA, never mind win a slam dunk contest? To the general public, *no*! But not to Spud Webb. He clearly believed in himself, and he did not listen to the naysayers along his life's journey.

Was it likely that a woman who had had five miscarriages, multiple years of no pregnancies, three IUI cycles, five IVF cycles (which included thirty-seven oocytes retrieved and eleven embryos transferred, with only one pregnancy that resulted in a tubal pregnancy and removal of one tube), and who had a grapefruit-size mesothelial cyst removed from her abdomen would ever go on to conceive a child naturally? Well, as you now know, crazier things do indeed happen! And yes, it was possible for me, not because it was likely, or because it was not, but because I truly followed my gut and heart, and I believed it was possible.

Life is full of synchronicities and blessings! Life is full of love, and loss is a part of loving. But our attitudes come from our beliefs about and feelings of things that shape our attitudes. We can change our attitudes and beliefs if we want to! We can be sad because something is gone, or we can be thankful that it happened. Along with the good, it is inevitable that there will be some bad, for it is out of the contrast that we gain clarity. Also, nothing is inherently good or bad, it is the meaning we attach to the circumstance that makes it good or bad. The same circumstance can be good for one person and bad for another. Abraham Hicks often says, "You can't know what you do want without knowing what you do not want." If we can look at what is not wanted more like the indicator that it is—not as a self-condemnation of how wrong we are or how badly we've screwed up, but just as an indicator of where we were at that moment—knowing it is totally within our power to change this at any moment, we will come into our true power of being the full spiritual human beings we are meant to be.

I was drawn to write this book at this precise moment in time. At the initial time of writing, my oldest son was turning twenty-four. My husband and I celebrated our twenty-fifth wedding anniversary, which was on the day after the book submission deadline for the writer's workshop I participated in that inspired me to tell my story. I normally would be so busy working that I would have found it hard to find the time to write this book. But it was during the COVID-19 pandemic that I had time and took the online writer's workshop and felt so drawn to finally write this book that I had started about twenty-one years ago. I first wrote the part of Joseph's story when he was three years old, and it is still on the FOD support website, https://www.fodsupport.org . The gift of COVID-19 was time, time to slow down my life and spend it with family, and to hear my inner calling.

I do realize many people lost loved ones during this time, and I do not mean to be insensitive to that. I do give those who have gone through loss my deepest condolences. I hope you can look back and have fond memories. And when you start to feel sad, flip the feeling to having appreciation that they happened, and I dare you to try and avoid the smile that comes across your face! For me, this time was a gift to simplify life and realize that the little things in life are what mean the most. The smile or touch of a loved one. Family game night. Family walks on the beach. Finding heart stones at the beach, and smiling up at the stars because I know the love that I was given in this life lasts forever. Laughing at life and finding the good in all things. Reaching for our individual heart-pounding, exciting, really big, difference-making dreams, because they are possible. And smiling at the synchronicities of life, like the fact that this book submission deadline was the day before the date of our "famiversary," April 20. This was just another sign that this was meant to be, and that I am supposed to share my story to help others.

The reason my husband and I had chosen this date for our wedding was that we had wanted to get married soon after our engagement, and we were at a party and spoke with my sister-in-law's in-laws and found out it was their wedding date. They had been married for a long time and had a great relationship, so we thought it was a good date to choose. After the fact, we found out it was Hitler's birthday, and subsequently, the reason for Columbine, the horrific school shooting. The boys who carried out this horrific attack chose this date because it was Hitler's birthday. And then it became "weed day," for some reason.

So we could focus on the fact that we chose Hitler's birthday—and the date of one of the most horrific mass shootings in our country and "weed day"—as our wedding date, or we could choose the fact that it was the same date as a wonderful couple who we could only hope to emulate and who had also chosen this day for their wedding date. On every given day, there are positive or negative things to focus on. We could choose to focus on it being our wedding date, or the day Joe got so sick. We could focus on him almost dying, or the fact that he lived. It's all opposite sides of the same coin. Where do you choose to put your focus and attention? Because that will decide how you experience this journey of life.

If I can give a little hope and love to someone and inspire them to follow their inner voice, then that is what I want. You need only ask yourself one thing: *Am I living my own truth, or someone else's belief of what my truth should be? Am I living from love, or from fear?* (OK, I know that was two questions.) I hope I have inspired you to go live your life from love, and to learn to trust yourself and your own inner spirit. My hope in writing this book is that the reader will find their own path to listen to their inner voice, because it has your best interest at heart, and to inspire others to look for hope, love, and your very own heart stones along your life's journey, because they are always there for you, you only need look for them!

"A Mother's Love Knows No Bounds"

From the first moment when you hold
a tiny babe in your arms and smile
through tears of tender emotions
until you draw your final breath

a Mother's love knows no bounds

even through the difficult times
your arms will always be open

because A Mother's love knows no bounds

Love is forever, and love, by definition, never changes. It cannot die, and therefore, love is all that is real! Love knows no bounds, especially a mother's love. A mother's love transcends all things, even this physical life! As I close my eyes, I can still feel my mother's love, and I am so thankful for her, and I know she lives on through me and my children. I know one day my children will have to live on without me in this physical realm, and I, too, will send them their own heart stones to show them I am always with them, even when I am gone from this earthly place. I hope for them that they always follow their hearts and stay true to themselves, and if things are not going the way they think they should, I hope they will take a step back, focus on the positive, and get quiet so they can hear their own inner voice because it is always speaking to them. They only need to listen for it.

Albert Einstein once said, "There are two ways to live your life. One is as though nothing is a miracle. The other is as though everything is a miracle." The only difference between these two approaches to life is how one thinks about life. I can guarantee this perspective in thought will make a world of difference to the people who live it. One will have a positive life, though not a problem-free life. However, with the mindset that everything is a miracle, one will be able to face those situations and move past them, never spending valuable time living in the space of the problem. By doing so, they become solution-oriented.

When you can do nothing about a situation, you can change your attitude toward it, and this will be the key to living a successful and happy life. I want my children to know that true success is measured in happiness, not in dollars, but as my oldest child so wisely once told us, he heard this saying from an anonymous source: "Money can't buy you happiness, but it can buy you a jet ski. Have you ever seen a sad guy on a jet ski?"

This always makes me laugh and smile, and he has a point! I want my children to have happiness and money, to be abundant in all areas of life, because they deserve the best in life; everyone does. But our beliefs about what we deserve can limit our abundance or allow it to flourish. We did not come here to survive. We came here to thrive. What is capable for one is possible for all, and even if no one has ever done it, and it seems like a crazy thing, and no one else believes in you, believe in yourself.

I wish for my children all the blessings of life, and Rascal Flatts's song, "My Wish," sums up all my hopes and dreams for them. I wish for them to always know that my husband and I, along with Spirit, are in their corner and love them. To make choices that are right for them, and for the dreams they want to come true. I want them to know that there is always another avenue or window to try to get where they want to go. That they know failing and making mistakes is part of the journey. That giving to others is the sweetest blessing of life. I wish for them to enjoy the journey, for the journey is the destination, and as long as they are having fun and loving life along the way, it doesn't really matter where they are going or where they end up. Because it's all good! God's love and grace is always with them, and their big dreams can and will come true. Let the worries go, and focus on letting life show them the big picture. They will have setbacks and challenges, but they will only serve to make the victories that much sweeter! And to savor the slow moments because life goes way too fast. To enjoy the precious, present moment is truly the best gift of life, for the present moment is all we ever have. Right here and now. Yesterday is gone, we can't change it. Tomorrow is yet to be, and it is not promised. Right now is all any of us ever have. Choose to be happy. Always live in the now! And, for crying out loud, have an amazing, adventurous, joy-filled ride on this fabulous road of life!

Being a mother has been the biggest blessing and gift of my life. To be a model of reaching for my dreams and never giving up is a role I do not take lightly, and I feel so blessed to have been given that role. To have fun, enjoy life, and have life become all that they want it to be, that is my ultimate dream for my children, and for that matter, for anyone who reads my story. To keep dreaming big, follow their hearts, and to know somebody always loves them and wants for them whatever they want for themselves, that is my message. My children are my greatest joy, ever! I hope they continue to find the blessings in all things and know that this is possible, even during the most difficult of circumstances. My dream was, and still is, my children.

When I was younger, I did not dream of being a teacher, an author, a designer, or a builder. My dream was to be a mom, and I get to live my dream every day. I am truly the most blessed person on earth! To share my story with others in the hopes of inspiring them to live their most authentic version of themselves is also a blessing. I hope through sharing my journey I can inspire others to be thankful for what they have while at the same time always reaching not for what is probable or realistic but for what is possible! Life is a miracle, and our possibilities are only limited by our imagination of them, but with hope and love and belief in yourself, anything is possible, even miracles. It is our belief in the extraordinary possibility of the everyday miracles to happen in all things, the expectation of blessed synchronicities, that allows them to happen and creates this wonderful, blessed journey called life! Because, in life, we all know now that crazier things have happened!

# Photos

I have included pictures of many heart-shaped objects and the angel cloud mentioned in my book. I think it is fun to show concrete evidence of spiritual happenings that cannot be explained away when seen with the eye.

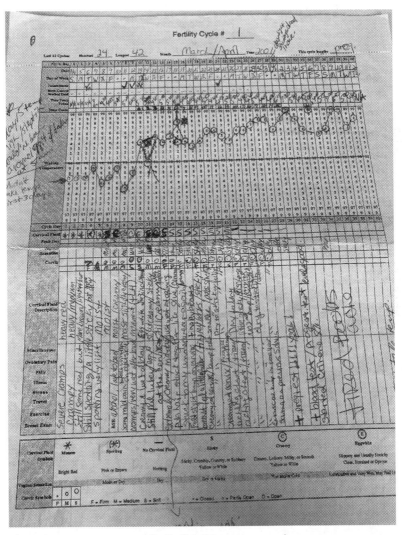

When I got pregnant with Colby. You can see the temperature stays way above the line after day twenty-eight, indicating pregnancy.

This is the picture of the angel in the clouds at
Colby's soccer game. Do you see her?

Heart shapes that show up in my life:

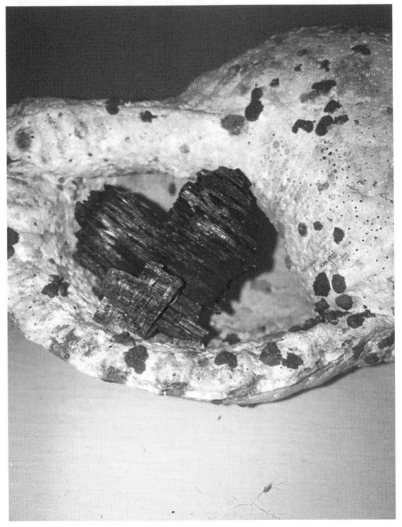

Two heart-shaped pieces of coal found at different times. The larger
one was found when I was cleaning the soot from the fireplace, and
it was just there. And then, at a completely different time, I was
putting the soot in a garbage bag, but it was still too hot and had
burned a hole in the bag, and the smaller one fell out onto the floor.

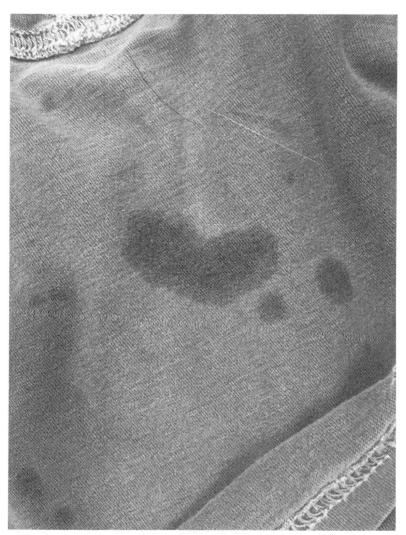

A heart-shaped wet spot on a pair of jeans.

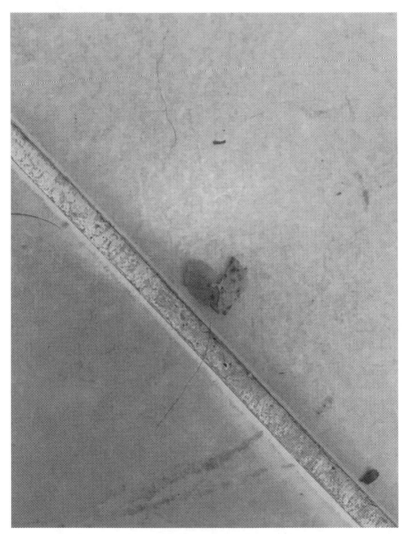

A tiny leaf on my floor.

A rock in the ground in the front of my side yard,
right under where we have a swing.

I literally have hundreds! This is just a small sample.

This one was too big to carry home!

An M&M, and yes, I still ate it!

A heart-shaped paint splatter on the sidewalk,
which I noticed while waiting for a ferry!

A heart-shaped potato skin from the bag of potatoes that somehow got stuck on the water bottles. I can't make this shit up!

# BOOKS OF INTEREST

Here is a list of books that I have found helpful, whether it was with fertility issues, life after the loss of a loved one, or on spirituality and synchronicities of life and going beyond and into the quantum.

Fertility:
>*Inconceivable* Julia Indichova
>*The Infertility Cure*, Randine Lewis, PhD
>*Fertility and Conception*, Zita West

After-Life/Loss:
>*The Light between Us*, Laura Lynne Jackson
>*Signs*, Laura Lynne Jackson
>*Second Firsts*, Christina Rasmussen
>Synchronicity, Chris Mackey
>*Dying To Be Me*, Anita Moorjani

Spirituality/Personal Development:
>*Ask and It Is Given*, Esther Hicks and Jerry Hicks (Abraham Hicks)
>*The Law of Attraction*, Esther Hicks and Jerry Hicks
>*The Biology of Belief*, Bruce Lipton, PhD
>*The Power of Intention*, Wayne Dyer
>*Wishes Fulfilled*, Wayne Dyer
>*Breaking the Habit of Being Yourself*, Dr. Joe Dispenza
>*You Are the Placebo*, Dr. Joe Dispenza
>*Becoming Supernatural*, Dr. Joe Dispenza

The above books have helped me open my heart and mind to other ways of looking at things in my life, whether it was how to take care of my body, my mind, my soul, or all three. We all will face challenges throughout our lives. Seeking the knowledge of someone who has been there already can prove very helpful in navigating our way. It allows us to figure out what is not just believable for someone else, but that when something is possible for someone else, it shifts our understanding and perception to realize it is also possible for ourselves.

What is possible for one is possible for everyone!

Love and blessings,
Stacey Webber

# ABOUT THE AUTHOR

Stacey Webber is a loving wife and mother who resides in New England. She has spent the last 25 years parenting and was also a pre-school teacher for more than 16 years. Motherhood did not come easily for her. She has experienced many forms of fertility treatments and was pregnant for the better part of ten years. She has had five miscarriages, multiple years of no pregnancies, three failed IUI cycles, five failed IVF cycles which included 37 oocytes (it's a fancy word for eggs) retrieved, and 11 embryos transferred into her uterus with only one resulting in a tubal pregnancy. This is her story of learning how her own beliefs were shaping her life and how in letting go of, trusting in, and living from love, all that was possible for her, and is possible for anyone.

Printed in the United States
by Baker & Taylor Publisher Services